Stores
of the Year
No.18

Stores
of the Year

No. 18

Martin M. Pegler

RSD Publishing, Inc., 302 Fifth Avenue, New York, NY

RSD Publishing, Inc.
302 Fifth Avenue
New York, NY 10001
212-279-7000
CS@rsdpublishing.com
www.rsdpublishing.com

Distributors to the trade in the United States and Canada
Innovative Logistics
575 Prospect Street
Lakewood NJ 08701
732-363-5679

Distributors outside the United States and Canada
HarperCollins International
10 East 53rd Street
New York, NY 10022-5299

Library of Congress Cataloging in Publication Data:
Stores of the Year No. 18

Printed and Bound in Hong Kong
ISBN: 978-0-9826128-7-3

TABLE OF CONTENTS

GLOBALSHOP

Sponsored by: A·R·E

GlobalShop is your annual connection to the retail design industry.

At the industry's largest annual event, meet more than 600 suppliers in one place—with the newest innovations to make your retail environment successful. Through education and networking you'll discover real-world solutions to enhance the retail experience and connect with the changing shopper.

GLOBALSHOP.ORG

GlobalShop 2012
February 29 – March 2
Las Vegas
Sands Expo & Convention Center

GlobalShop 2013
April 16 – 18
Chicago
McCormick Place

INTRODUCTION

With each edition of *Stores of the Year* we become more international and more and more the retail shops, stores and boutiques we present represent more and more of the world. It is not that the world is getting smaller, rather it is that our grasp of the retail scene has become more inclusive. As we mature and with the aid of the internet and you our readers, we are being introduced to new projects in faraway lands and new architects and store designers who are generous enough to share the fruits of their talents with us.

If the reader has a number of past volumes of *Stores of the Year* on his or her library shelf — and we are pleased to note that so many of you are actually "collectors" (and even go hunting on eBay for missing editions to fill in the gaps) — if you look back to the earlier volumes they were almost exclusively about what was happening in retail design in the 1980s and early 1990s. That was a time when study groups of retailers and designers from Asia — first an influx from Japan, then from South Korea — made trips to the U.S. to study what we were doing — how we were doing what we were doing — and with what and why. As a Visual Merchandise person, I was invited to Japan, South Korea, Singapore, Koala Lampur and Indonesia to share my knowledge with these developing retailers. Now, if you look at the Table of Contents of *Stores of the Year 18* you will see that we have included retail spaces from UAE, China, India, South Korea, The Philippines and Poland mixed in with those from the United Kingdom, Germany, Austria, Switzerland, Spain, Canada and the United States. This is a mixed bag and we are proud of how international this "mix" is. Together, these *Stores of the Year* books are a "history of retail design."

Though the stores represent a "retail United Nations," the designers and architects whose projects we are showing are almost as diverse as the places where they are working. Japanese store designers who once looked to the U.S. for information and possibly direction are now pointing the way for others and designing stores in the States. British and German design firms are creating the local retail experiences in UAE and Dubai — fully cognizant of the local traditions, customs and taboos. Today's architects and designers are the ambassadors of good will spreading the "retail glad tidings" and offering up universal style and sophistication while aware and respectful of the local cultures and traditions. These designers are like the honey gathering bees that go from flower to flower not only leaving traces of their knowledge and expertise but also absorbing ideas that they carry away with them to deposit in another country and another culture. Also we are seeing the advancement of "local talent" — the native born architects and designers who are creating the retail stores that combine what is best of their culture with what is happening design-wise around the world. We are pleased to have included the projects of new native talents from The Philippines and India in this volume.

As the reader peruses this book, he or she will note that some stores are stamped or overlaid with elements that make the design site-specific to a particular country. But, many shops are designed so they can be lifted out of a mall in one country and dropped intact into a mall continents away. These stores would still be right and fitting and be right at home because the design was targeted at a specific market — a specific age group or lifestyle. Young, trendy and fashion-aware shoppers in China, India, South Korea and The Philippines are just as tuned in as their comparable group in the U.S. or the U.K. They see the same movies, listen to the same music, tweet and connect by cell phones and respond to the same or similar views on YouTube and thus, aside for maybe local taboos, can be approached in the same way.

So, as in the past, we invite you to sit back, relax and enjoy this trip around the world of retail. There are no extra charges for luggage — no waiting shoeless in line to go through customs — no passports to stamp — and pick the seat of your choice. As the captain for this voyage and the editor of *Stores of the Year* — "Bon Voyage" and have an enjoyable and enlightening trip.

Martin M. Pegler

Shinsegae Chungcheong
Cheonan, South Korea

DESIGN
CBX Retail Division, New York, NY
JMCBX, South Korea

PRESIDENT, CBX RETAIL DIVISION
Joseph Bona

MANAGING DIRECTOR, JMCBX/CBX TEAM
Joon Kyu Whang

CREATIVE DIRECTOR, CBX RETAIL DIVISION
Peter Burgoyne

PHOTOGRAPHY
Yawoori-Cheonan (owner)

Peter Burgoyne, Creative Director at CBX Retail Division, the design firm for this new, free-standing department store in Cheonan, South Korea, was challenged by the client "to create a luxurious shopping environment that reflects the classic minimalism of the Shinsegae heritage, but also to create a new destination and brand assortment for the young active customer of Cheonan [50 miles south of Seoul] within the west building [of the new store]. Additionally, by blending in an unusual third element, the Arrario Gallery, art will be curated in and around the store to create a unique shopping experience."

The first wing, of what will eventually be a 495,900 sq.

ft. two-winged store, is now open and shown here. It expands over 287,900 sq. ft.; later this year the 193,900 sq. ft. second wing is scheduled to open. Joseph Bona, President of CBX Retail Division says that the new design is different from the Centum City flagship store but "it is consistent with the company's established classic minimalism aesthetic." Peter Burgoyne adds that, "the special amenities found inside the Chungcheong store — such as the Culture Hall, the rooftop garden, and the VIP lounges are more in keeping with features found in a hospitality environment and are destined to appeal to customers of all ages."

The new store carries a wide range of product geared to this market's "upper-income and aspirational" shoppers. All this is set in an ambiance of neutral colors ranging from warm and bright whites through a variety of gray tones to cool ebony. The colors are complemented by the metal finishes, stone, marble, glass and the deep pile carpets. Adding different, distinct looks to the various departments are the assorted ceiling treatments. There are the sweeping curved soffits and circular ripple-like coves in the women's area, the deconstructed tree canopies in the children's department, the vaulted ceiling in cosmetics and a spectacular curved domed ceiling atop the east void. Also defining the wing is the central atrium which allows an abundance of natural light into the space and complements the energy-saving lighting plan that includes LED, metal halides and fluorescent fixtures.

CBX also handled traffic circulation and departmental adjacency planning in Shinsegae's multiple buildings and levels. These include the new passageways that will seamlessly connect the selling areas that will eventually be divided between the east and west buildings. Special art and display areas have been created within "many of the architectural transitions arising from the complicated building conditions. Technology is used in the children's area to create interactive displays. Peter Burgoyne adds, "Visual

merchandising followed the narrative developed to inform all the design decisions throughout the project. Using the three elements of Cheonan's 'fast paced moving river,' Cheonan; the 'natural elegance and beauty' of Shinsegae; and Arrario's 'winds of art and fashion,' key areas within the public space receive large category-defining and seasonal VM presentations in keeping with the scale of the store. Large sculptural installations within the west atrium and art curated atop the roof garden become additional manifestations of the VM program within this vast space."

Joon Kyu Whang, Managing Director of the JMCBX/ CBX design team served as the lead contact on the Chungcheung project and was instrumental in the design direction and adapted global design standards to the local Korean market. Whang said, "With this new store in Cheonan, Shinsegae will now compete with the country's other luxury merchants in a new environment designed especially for this market's more affluent and aspirational customers, with all the amenities they expect and require. We also have an opportunity to engage younger customers through appealing public spaces and the latest trend merchandise."

SM Department Stores

Cubao and Fairview, Philippines

DESIGN
Point Design, New York, NY/Makati City, Philippines

CREATIVE DIRECTOR
Diego Garay

PRINCIPAL IN CHARGE
Leandro Artigala

Design Team at SM Cubao
PROJECT MANAGEMENT
Catalina Rojas

DESIGNERS
Gwendolyn Flores, Akinori Okada, Ignacio Cristofori, Marina Cristofori

Design Team at SM Fairview
PROJECT MANAGEMENT
Leo Lotopolsky, Brigida Squassi

PROJECT COORDINATOR
Cecilia Cambeses

DESIGNERS
Marina Cristofori, Ignacio Cristofori, Cora Garone, Daniel Nazareno

GRAPHIC DESIGN
Clementina Koppmann, Dolores Arenaza

PHOTOGRAPHER
Lito Lopez

When we receive a job description for a project that makes for interesting reading, we present the material with very little editing for our readers to enjoy. We were truly delighted when the people at Point Design of New York City and the Philippines sent us this project and the following information about its genesis. We hope you find the text illuminating and educational.

Romancing the Store
SM Department Stores Get More than a Usual Face-lift

Let's face it, there's much more to shopping than just the simple act of making a purchase. In truth, it's like a game of seduction, one that involves attraction and flattery. And in our consumer society, shopping is such a routine activity, it is deeply ingrained in our consciousness. In fact, there's really no boundary between it and the rest of our lives. But where you shop, what seduces you specifically, and how that becomes part of your day-to-day life, says a lot about who you are.

Retailers recognize this fact. They spend lots of time and money identifying their customers' desires and aspirations, and figuring out how they can satisfy them. Of course, this comes down to merchandise and to environments that create shopping experiences that appeal to particular customers. As in any game of seduction, the most attractive and engaging player wins, and this fight for consumer attention and loyalty extends across the board, from small concept shops to established retail giants.

When Merchandise Was King
Department stores of the 19th and 20th centuries capitalized on their role as one-stop shops — places where customers could find a great variety of merchandise in different categories and price points all under one roof. In those days, the choice of goods was enough to attract customers and keep them loyal.

Fast forward to the present. The novelty of the large retail hub faded long ago, yet department stores persist. Shoppers still look to them for all-in-one service and convenience. But they also look to the vast numbers of specialty retailers that have appeared, and these relative newcomers (in every shape and size) have drawn sizable market share from their vener-

able, trusted forebears. What are department stores to do?

Clearly, they can no longer rely on their variety of merchandise alone. They have to stay relevant and responsive — which means they've got to meet consumer demand for something new, fresh and attractive. At all times. To succeed, department stores have to invest in creating shopping experiences that speak to their clientele. No longer is it enough to remodel stores every four to six years — the norm for many stores in Asia. They've got to move much more quickly than that.

Breaking New Ground in the Philippines

In the Philippines, where shopping is considered a form of recreation and entertainment, department stores and malls are gathering places. People listen to the buzz, and go to the venues that offer the most fun, excitement and distinctive shopping experiences. When Shoe Mart (SM), the country's largest department store chain, recognized this new reality, their stores hadn't been updated in more than five years. But rather than simply modernize interiors, SM jumped at the opportunity to revitalize their brand, using the shopping environment itself as a critical element in appealing to customers new and old.

Originally a shoe store founded more than a half-century ago by Henry Sy, SM eventually developed into a full-line department store. Today the chain encompasses 40 branch stores and malls strategically located in Manila and in key cities around the Philippines. Long years in the business have made SM a significant player in the country's mass-market retail arena, catering largely to a lower-middle-market clientele. With the revitalization program,

management has set its sights on a slightly higher-level customer, without wishing to alienate its existing base. To address these complex issues, SM brought in Point Design Inc., the New York-based retail-design firm headed up by Diego Garay, AIA, a well-known architect and designer. Starting with the Ortigas store (SM Megamall) in 2005, Point's team set out to redesign the stores, giving them a more fun and sophisticated look and feel.

Point's Big Design Appeal

SM knew what they were getting when they chose Point to help them energize their brand. Teresita Sy-Coson, SM's president for retail, was familiar with the firm's award-winning work in TSUM's Moscow flagship store, one of the highest-end department stores in Europe, and a leader in the hot Russian retail market. "She liked the simplicity of the design and thought the fixtures were beautiful," says Allen Felsenthal, Point Design principal and managing director for Asia. "However, she also knows that SM is in an entirely different market from TSUM," adds Diego Garay. "She was basically inspired by the design's simplicity, efficiency and sophistication. It was done with great taste in a minimalist manner."

The challenge for Point was, in part, to adapt high-end solutions to suit the developing Philippine market. "Filipinos are value-seekers and are very aware of trends. The majority may not be able to afford them, but they know what a good buy is. Plus they always aspire to more," Diego explains. To create a whole new experience for customers, the new store design offers a sophisticated shopping environment and a line of fashionable, yet affordable

merchandise aimed at making Filipino shoppers feel and look good.

Point Design introduced three major improvements to revamp SM's shopping environment and shoppers' experience. First, they revisited the basic layout of merchandise. While categories were thoughtfully grouped and laid out, the distance within individual departments from aisle to back wall was too deep. "The problem with deep sections is that customers can't immediately see the merchandise from the aisle. This creates a boomerang effect, with customers turning back to the aisle from the middle of the department, and missing a good deal of merchandise on offer," explains Leandro Artigala, Point Design principal. "With the new plan, we made departments shallower, the aisles wider and the merchandise much more visible. Shoppers can find the items they're looking for."

Second, a more dramatic lighting scheme replaced flat, bright fluorescent lighting. While Point was aiming for a more theatrical effect — employing an interplay of light and shade, the design team had to make sure the stores would be bright enough. "When we started the project with SM, everything looked flat mostly because the lighting was flat," Leandro continues. "When it comes to lighting these stores, we were challenged to find the right balance between a compelling composition with dramatic lighting, and the Filipino shopper's general preference for bright spaces." Point solved this with ceiling coves and recessed downlights that provide general lighting and add powerful lines and patterns to the ceiling. The design also provides spotlights and directional highlights to guide customers to featured areas and items. For dramatic effect, LED chandeliers by the escalator well provide a visual attraction to the open, vertical space. The mix of highlights and lowlights adds dimension and texture and makes the merchandise look appealing.

Finally, the new stores made the most of interesting materials in an array of forms, patterns and colors, offering creative solutions that worked within a very tight budget. Leandro says, "Presented with the budget, we immediately saw an opportunity to think outside of the box in terms of the materials we could choose and how we could use less expensive finishes to achieve an exciting, smart look." Special attention was paid to flooring, which can play into a customer's sense of whether a store is good or bad. Designs called for pricier ceramic and glass mosaic tile in the aisles, which are most visible to customers. Color and pattern make them interesting and help minimize both their monotony and length. In the merchandise departments, Point used more economical vinyl tiles — a material that has improved dramatically in the last decade, in a dark wood finish, which contrasts nicely with the light-colored aisles and makes the departments pop.

The new store designs also played with graphics for added color, pattern and visual texture at manageable cost. "We picked patterns from the 1950s and 60s associated with high-end design, and digitally converted them into wallpaper and graphic stickers for the walls and ceilings," says Leandro. "Where possible, we chose less expen-

sive materials like vinyl and wallpaper in place of fabric or real wood to make the store look chic without breaking the bank." And the finishes definitely appeal to the Filipino love of color and texture.

Environments that Sell

Point Design's newly conceptualized SM Department Stores now sport a fresh, sophisticated and exciting design that offers a hard-working platform for merchandise. Bright colors combine with dramatic lighting to give the stores' wares greater appeal, and attract customers to explore and spend time in their vibrant spaces. Though designed primarily to move goods, SM's playful, fashionable environments also, importantly, make customers feel good

and the shopping experience enjoyable. And while customers can feel excited about the new design, they're also reminded that SM remains the store they've come to know and count on all these years.

For Point, the design process for SM was unlike others, as they tended to work backwards on these projects. "Normally, a client would say, 'I plan to sell Prada or Gucci or Ray-Ban.' In response," explains Diego, "we create an environment suited to sell that type of merchandise. But with SM, we moved the design to a higher-end look while maintaining the same merchandise lines. Because the environment is telling customers they can spend more, high-ticket items started selling more. As lower-end items began selling less, SM started bringing in better brands. The

store observes how people respond to the new look, and follows up with higher-end merchandise."

Since work on the first store, Ortigas in SM Megamall, Point Design has gone on to renovate several other sites, including SM Cubao, SM Fairview and SM Pampanga. Though elements of the design are prototypical, employed in each location, each store is different, featuring colors, decorative details and lighting to suit its specific market. The Point Design team is proud of the fact that their designs for SM not only look great, but also make shopping easier and more fun for customers — and have increased sales. "We are a firm that understands retail very, very well, and that's why we are able to solve design problems with precision, whether the store caters to a high-end mar-

ket like TSUM or to the mid-market like SM," says Diego.

And succeeding in retail, be it design or sales, is no easy feat. "Retail design is complex, and perhaps more so than any other design discipline," Diego explains. "As Ken Walker, founder of retail design firm Walker Group/CNI where Allen and I came from, would say, one can compare retail design to a hamburger wherein all the ingredients need to be right for the experience to be right, simply because you eat them all at once. If one of the ingredients is bad, the hamburger is bad. In retail, if you miss one thing, the project won't be right. Each element has to be done correctly because one element cannot compensate for any other."

Saks Fifth Avenue Designer Floor

Fifth Ave., New York, NY

DESIGN
Mancini Duffy, New York, NY

CREATIVE DIRECTOR
Edward Calabrese

DIRECTOR OF CREATIVE RESOURCES
Lisa Contreras

PROJECT DIRECTOR/PLANNER
Michael L. Kim

FOR SAKS FIFTH AVENUE
VP STORE DESIGN & CONSTRUCTION
William Herbst, Sr.

VP STORE DESIGN
Marco Oppici

VP STORE PLANNING
Errol Pierre

LIGHTING DESIGN
Doug Russell of Lighting Workshop

GENERAL CONTRACTOR
Tri-Con Construction, Bensalem, PA

ARCHITECTS OF RECORD
Bridges & Lavin Architects

PHOTOGRAPHY
Courtesy of Mancini Duffy, Adrian Wilson

Larger than many stores is the newly renovated and re-planned 50,000 sq. ft. designer's floor in Saks Fifth Avenue in New York City. This newly opened Designer's Floor now houses almost 50 world renowned designer collections some of which are presented in their own individual "boutiques" on this floor. The roll call of designers located in specific spaces range from Acres, Alexander McQueen and Chanel through the haute couture alphabet up through Valentino, Versace and Yves St. Laurent. Though the new floor was designed by Mancini Duffy of New York City, the Louis Vuitton collection is set off in a special setting designed by Peter Marino. The central floor area has been turned over to "rising designers" and new talents.

Edward Calabrese, Creative Director at Mancini Duffy said, "This was a true collaboration between Saks creative team and Mancini Duffy. The executive committee was extremely sensitive to how other designer spaces and stores with multiple vendor shops were handled — they did not want a white generic box or an uninteresting assembly of store fronts." What evolved, according to Calabrese, was "a simple architecture but purposefully interrupted with 'moments' and 'highlight' areas. The Saks architecture of ceiling and shop fronts and aisle systems took on a richness of texture and detail of its own that was at least equal to the strength of the various designer shop designs." Thus, on this open, airy and spacious floor with its striated marble aisles and weathered oak flooring topped with decorative area rugs from Tibet made of wool and silk, its special carved glass panels and textured cream colored Venetian plaster walls — the Saks brand shines through.

"Rich materials were selected and designed that expressed a 'hand tooled' feel," says Calabrese. In addition to the afore-

mentioned Venetian plaster surfaced surround walls there are sculptural carved glass and gold filigree panels as well as "special faux bois etched bronze mirrors that contrast with flat 'torn paper plaster' on the elevator surround. Some areas are highlighted with copper wall covering panels and a statuary bronze finish was used for all fixtures for "its richness and warmth. A very carefully orchestrated palette of contrasting textures was created."

In addition to the wealth of designer names, the space is enhanced with art work that adds another layer of luxury to the setting. Gold filigree panels and unique chandeliers were commissioned and executed by Michele Oka Doner and a Zaha Hadid table, the focal point in the central area,

contrasts "hand tooled texture with a smooth sculptural quality."

Doug Russell of Lighting Workshop created the ambient lighting plan, carefully blending the lighting for the aisles with several areas that "pop" and other areas that are intentionally softer. Since some of the individual boutiques created their own lighting effects, Russell had to do "a very careful calculation of all the combined effects."

Summing up the look of the floor, Edward Calabrese said, "The floor expresses a new sense of luxury which is really expressed in a sense of spaciousness, interesting finishes and materials. It is a space that is welcoming and offers many spaces to explore."

Jelmoli
Bahnhofstrasse, Zurich, Switzerland

ARCHITECT/DESIGNER:
Blocher Blocher Partners, Stuttgart, Germany

PHOTOGRAPHY:
Courtesy of Blocher Blocher Partners

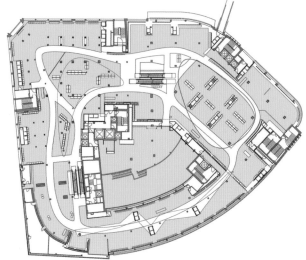

In presenting the award for achievement in Retail Design 2011 at Euroshop in Dusseldorf, the presenter of the award said the following.

"It is one of the best known and long established addresses in downtown Zurich. It is a department store which was already founded in the 19th century and which at all times was always very successful in reinventing itself and responding to the changes in consumer behavior. So they changed very early from a traditional department store to 'The House of Brands'"

And — the winner was and is Jelmoli, who after extensive renovations presented its new look to the world. The architects/designers of the renovations to the men's and women's floors is the award winning architectural firm in Stuttgart — Blocher Blocher Partners.

As one would expect in such large spaces (3000 sq. meters in the women's area and 4000 sq. meters on the men's floor) there are numerous products and brands on view. However, the judges credited "minimalism and transparency" in the design for some of the success of the new look. Also, "the distinguished ambience of the refurbished departments is composed of an appealing mix of the most varied and exquisite materials. Abstractedly designed mid-floor walls of perforated metal and an exclusive wall design of special 'concrete surface' are prominent." In the men's department "unusual used-look oak furniture, high quality curtains and impressive, large, transparent glass walls immediately catch the observer's eye."

The women's floor (the second) proves that Jelmoli is "The House of Brands" with over 100 of the world's most noted brands and designers represented. Ranging from jeans and sportswear to evening fashions, the architects/designers created a "boulevard" for strolling and seeing — provided with "ambience and charisma." Or, as the Jelmoli spokesperson describes it, "Jelmoli knows how to place various brands and labels in a scene so that they can unfold their power and personality." Menswear appears on the first floor along with children's wear and shoes for both men and women. Here one will find casual wear as well as suits for men and accessories.

Hanspeter Gruninger, the Store Manager of Jelmoli, took over that position and was very involved in realizing the new concept/look of the store. He said, "We need a house that is still going to work well in 10 years and that will play an even more prominent part in the years to come. We have examples showing us that being a normal department store is really not sufficient anymore. The goal is to present the lifestyle and sports world on an even broader scale and to complement them with new, exclusive brands. That is where we see our future and that is the path we will take."

With this stunning new store design Jelmoli is definitely on its way to being as it hopes to be, a "Premium Power Fashion House of Tomorrow."

Iconic
Dubai, U.A.R.

DESIGN
SFD, London, UK

JOINT MANAGING DIRECTOR
Paul Brooks

CREATIVE DIRECTOR
Andi Grant

DESIGN
Dalziel and Pow Design Consultants,
London, UK

CREATIVE DIRECTOR
David Dalziel

TEAM LEADER
Caroline Johnston

PHOTOGRAPHY
Andy Townsend

Something new and exciting is happening in Dubai, where new and exciting things seem to be the norm. This time it is the new department store, Iconic, jointly designed by SFD and Dalziel and Pow Design Consultants — both of London — for the Landmark Group. According to the designers: "The concept is a bold, confident lifestyle offer, aimed at a young, middle market." This market is under serviced in the region, where premium brands having dominated for so long. Spread over 5,600 sq. meters (almost 60,000 sq. ft.) on two floors, Iconic has taken over the former premium boutique shopping center in Dubai and has completely refinished it to be a fresh, fun, new experience for not-so-affluent shoppers. In addition to offering fashions for the family, the space includes a spa, a café, a restaurant and an all-important electronics department.

The overall concept was generated by SFD and that included all the departmental treatments, wall and floor fixtures, the visual merchandising and window displays. They also supplied, manufactured and installed much of the retail equipment, shopfitting, mannequins and propping. For their part, Dalziel and Pow designed the interior architecture, the planning and shell, as well as the detailed design of the spa and the restaurant. "Working in this way SFD and Dalziel and Pow have shared and combined their retail expertise to produce a truly unique retail experience."

Paul Brooks of SFD explains, "It was clear that the vision of the client was considering something that truly lived up to the Iconic name — with requirements for drama, surprise and excitement key to the brand ethos. The sheer size of the space and the range of offerings being considered were one of the key challenges to this project. It was vital to ensure that each departmental area came alive with an individual personality, whilst creating a cohesive experience across a range of merchandise values from high street to premium."

Iconic is a lifestyle destination for a particular market in retail ridden Dubai. According to the design team: "Each department has an intentionally distinctive identity,

but together they sit with a complementary look and feel — defining the entire space. All the shop-in-shop spaces share a similar aesthetic, but stand out within the concept. The architectural space is more neutral by comparison, with a single floor treatment punctuated by occasional highlights and a dark, exposed ceiling with suspended white rafts of various scales related to the departmental layout." The half height walls were instrumental in both separating areas and controlling the customers journey through the store — "providing a level of discovery and delight which is part of the Iconic retail experience," added Paul Brooks.

Setting the look for the space is the almost 40 ft. tall ceiling in the atrium with a central hanging installation of chromed shapes connecting the upper and lower floors visually. This central area with full height glass walls "is truly an iconic space and it is within this area that the iconic vision is fully realized." From the ICONIC lettering of the front window display to the blue trend ramp (the runway) and mannequins, hexagonal hanging installation, surrounded by LED screens and projections, "the space allows these elements to breathe without dividing attention from the merchandise offering at floor level. In addi-

tion, these features when viewed from the exterior provide a taste of the retail environment within." Some of the other special visual treats in the new store include the LED wall that frames the escalator as well as the strong, dramatic focal displays that highlight key areas or departments in the store. Among the unique looking shops contained in Iconic are footwear, accessories, denim, sport, casual and formals and — all together — they combine to create something that lives up to the "Iconic" name.

"The Iconic project was a unique opportunity to create an exciting new store as well as influence the development of a new brand from an early stage, this is a rare situation with many retail brands already established. As creative partners (SFD, Dalziel and Pow and the Landmark Group) there was a large degree of freedom given by Iconic to create something that was conceptually bold, fresh and innovative which was a great honor and challenge. The collaboration aspect was a key ingredient to the success of the project and the complementary skills of SFD, Dalziel and Pow and the Iconic team were instrumental in creating such a diverse and unique store," is how Paul Brooks summed up this achievement.

Christian Lacroix
East 57th Street, New York, NY

DESIGN
KREO Gallery, Paris, France
Under the direction of Christian Lacroix

CEO, FOUNDER
Clemence Krzentowski

PROJECT MANAGER
Charlotte Brosse

DESIGN
Pavlik Design Team, Ft. Lauderdale, FL

PRINCIPAL
Mark Hammil

PROJECT MANAGER
Diana Santiago

ARCHITECT
Anthony C. Baker AIA, FARA, New York, NY

PHOTOGRAPHY
Dana Hoff

This store, located on East 57th Street, between Fifth and Madison Avenues, is in the heart of the luxury retail scene in New York City. It is the first Christian Lacroix boutique in New York and only the second in the U.S. The first was a boutique in the Forum Shops in Las Vegas. For the New York store, the retailer called upon the Pavlik Design Team of Ft. Lauderdale to use their talents and expertise and adapt the original design concepts created by the Kreo Gallery of Paris working under the direction of Lacroix. Pavlik had to recreate Lacroix's vision — a shop with "the decorative energy of the French baroque and the crisp minimal lines of contemporary design."

The 1741 sq. ft. store continues the design concept in-

troduced in the Las Vegas boutique: the space is filled with color, patterns and numerous graphic details. The classic storefront is an elegant black color with an awning of the same color extending out to the curb for the carriage trade — those shoppers who arrive by limousine or taxi. From this gracious touch and through the large glazed display area shoppers get a full view into the store, dark but dramatically illuminated.

To fill the void in the higher ceiling area, a unique Murano glass chandelier/totem (designed by Lacroix) was used. This "totem" is enhanced by the numerous symbols associated with Lacroix such as the sun, the heart, and, of course, the color red.

The Pavlik designers were challenged by the long narrow footprint of the space,
the varying ceiling heights and the elevated room at the rear. The space was made to appear wider through the use of strategically placed mirrors. Amid the dark warm gray and black areas and surfaces in the shop there are brilliant accents of red as in the circular carpets topped with contemporary pouf seating, the shelves that seem to pop off the dark walls and the decorative hanging chandeliers.

Shoppers follow a signature red inlaid carpet to get to the elevated back room. The fixtures are inspired by 18th century French furniture styles and have lacquered finishes. Warm wenge wood flooring is used throughout and is complemented by the polished concrete walls and the bevel-edged mirror tiles. Some of the walls are covered

with a scene-scape of Lacroix's native Arles in a rustic print. Walnut veneered wall surfaces are printed with kaleidoscopic patterns created by Lacroix. The fitting rooms, at the rear, play old against new with modern chandeliers suspended from the plaster appliquéd ceiling trimmed with French crown moldings.

Christian Lacroix said, "I will never forget how supportive the U.S. and New York were at the very beginning of my career, so it is a legitimate return to my 'American roots' 20 years later — after my first show here." The new boutique has found a welcome home on East 57th Street surrounded by many other famous designer name boutiques.

Ermenegildo Zegna

Fifth Avenue, New York, NY

ARCHITECT/DESIGNER
Peter Marino, New York, NY

CONSTRUCTION
Shawmut Design & Construction, Boston, MA

PHOTOGRAPHY
Paul Warchol, New York, NY

The three story, 9200 sq. ft. Zegna boutique on Fifth Avenue in New York City has been completely redesigned and enlarged by Peter Marino, a New York City based architect/design firm. The international men's luxury clothing and accessory brand moved from its previous 6000 sq. ft. location to this new, larger one and according to the contractors, the Shawmut Design & Construction company of Boston, "The overall goal of creating a space to more accurately reflect their brand was accomplished through the unique use of materials and sculptural concepts. The Zegna spirit and brand story is reinforced through the use of noble materials, natural colors, tactile sensations and

technical innovations — all derived from Zegna's fabric heritage. A key inspiration for the store design was the original wool mill in Trivero, Italy which has made custom fabric for their [Zegna's] designs for nearly 100 years."

The store was designed to suggest a weaving loom in action. The 22 ft. tall glass entryway is made of 900 sq. ft. of continuous glass and from there stainless steel cables weave their way through the store. "The criss-crossing cables warp and weft in a strong literal reference to the horizontal and vertical yarns which make up the abstract notion of a swatch of fabric." Zegna's CashCo (a corduroy blend of cashmere and cotton) is reinterpreted in the stuc-

co wall treatment used on the passages between the floors. To suggest the signature yellow selvage of the Zegna fabrics, the golden yellow radica marble stripe appears from floor to wall. "These references to material texture and movement dominate a shopper's senses from the moment they walk past the storefront windows to the top floor."

Peter Marino, the designer, describes this store as "an elegant townhouse" where each floor, and each room on each floor, has "a different use and therefore a different atmosphere." The entry level is given over to shirts, ties, accessories and men's underwear. Dressy casual wear is on the second level while high-end suits and tuxes are on the third floor which comes furnished with a fireplace. "Each floor is modern and contemporary in feel and look, with elements that would appeal to a conservative taste as well."

In order to create the desired "masculine feel," Marino selected a brown/bronze color scheme to complement the stone, dark woods and steel of the palette. Mahogany, bleached oak and leather contrast with the sleekness of the glass, stained steel and the textured stone. The accent colors are the alpine green and sky blue that appear on the ground level in the mural behind the glass and steel staircase. The elaborate metal and glass staircase in the center of the store "showcases a nature mural which changes colors through a seasonal palette." The company's commitment to the environment has been respected and is evidenced in the use of the aforementioned sustainable raw materials. Another "nod to nature is the congruent theme of the store — conceptualized through the colors in the various rooms."

Of special note are the 19 different plaster finishes specified by Marino to affect the desired tactile experience. It is only one of the numerous details that make this new Fifth Avenue boutique a worthwhile shopping experience.

Moschino

West 14th Street, New York, NY

ARCHITECTURAL DESIGN
Vudafieri Partners & Mariotti Studio, Milan, Italy

INTERIOR DESIGN
Duexl

CONSTRUCTION AND INTERPRETATION
Shawmut Design & Construction, Boston, MA

PHOTOGRAPHY
Courtesy of Moschino, Milan, Italy

The former Quality Meats butcher shop in New York City's Meatpacking District — now a much touted and developed fashion center — presented a series of unique challenges to the Shawmut Design & Construction company of Boston. For one thing, they were required to reinterpret and execute the designs of the Milan architects Vudafieri Partners and Mariotti Studio and the interior design of Duexl; and, they had to make it work and conform to the NYC building codes. It also meant coordinating with the Italian designers to install the abstract flower prints — printed in Italy — on the white lacquered walls of the 14th Street location. In addition, the original floors of the space were uneven and unusable, so the Shawmut team had to reconstruct the floor with a new subfloor underneath of white composite stone.

This is the first U.S. Moschino store being built to this design concept which "brings to life the luxury designer's fairy tale theme and signature heart motif for the 'classic-with-a-twist' appeal." The first impression of the new design is of the 40-foot-long shopfront that features "fanciful, creative messages." These displays are changed every few months in the style of those used in Moschino's Milan windows which are noted for their attention getting and surprising details.

The interior presents "a luminous showcase of classic fixtures, reimagined to resemble surrealistic flora and fauna." Stainless steel is a key element in the store design and here it has been incorporated into tree shaped display

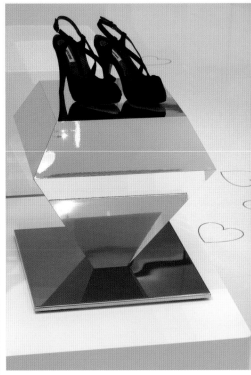

stands. The "fruit" that hangs from these "trees" are the various Moschino clothing lines including Moschino, Moschino Cheap and Chic, Love Moschino and Moschino Uomo. A Shawmut-coordinated, expert metal fabricator helped orchestrate the steel installation — including the stainless steel heart outlines that were inlaid into floor tiles in Italy and shipped to the site for installation.

The white marble tiled floor — with heart inlays — is covered in some areas with iridescent Lurex rugs that are embellished with plant and animal imagery to affect a warm contrast to the cool floors. Traditional Plexiglas teardrop lighting fixtures shaped into Moschino hearts shower down throughout the boutique. The red slipper chairs, sit-

uated throughout, are covered with dozens of stuffed felt hearts and carry the Moschino message as well. The unique jewelry cases are shaped like giant diamond rings.

"Hearts and flowers" is the story in this boutique that now adds another "must-see, must do" to the ever growing list of "what's new" in the Meatpacking District. Whimsy and fashion come together as Italian born designs have been interpreted and produced by an American construction/design firm for a new audience.

Boutique 1

Mirdif City Center, Dubai, UAR

DESIGN
Caulder Moore Consultancy, Kew, London, UK

CREATIVE DIRECTOR
Ian Caulder

DESIGN DIRECTOR
Maria Correia

SENIOR DESIGNER
David Cheney

PHOTOGRAPHY
Courtesy of Boutique 1

Located in the Mirdif City Center in Dubai in an 1100 sq. meter space (about 11,500 sq. ft.) is the new, luxurious Boutique 1. Designed for Ziad and Lena Matta and their upscale clientele by the Caulder Moore Design Consultancy, the space is filled with women's fashions by top designers like Missoni, Mulberry, Oscar de la Renta and Diane von Furstenberg as well as famous name-brands of menswear. In addition, there is a home accessories department, a book shop and a beauty salon.

Ian Caulder, the creative director of the design firm said, "The area counts many local residents and we wanted to appeal to them — giving them more reasons to pop in and discover new things on a regular basis. We gave the store a more relaxed, casual accessible feel with flexibility and plenty of opportunity to change and create new inspir-

ing visual merchandising that will attract regular visitors to the store. It is like an inspiring contemporary art gallery where the exhibits are the key focus and constantly changing."

The façade — all glass — is simple and asymmetrical, and some of the newest garments are featured on the white abstract mannequins in the open back windows. The massive columns, part of the construction," become individually sculptured art forms that can be viewed on entry to the store — reinforcing the effect of a contemporary art gallery. Accessories are presented to the right of the entry and a focal element here is a changeable platform that can be used as a single entity or broken up into a series of asymmetrical pieces. Mannequins are on show here and the set-up "adds energy and dynamism to the space and

reinforces the idea that things are constantly changing."
Behind this is a large display wall with a slanting mirror
and a try-on area that holds sculptural and colorful seating for those who attend the shoppers. Heralding the
women's fashion area, at the rear of the store, is a unit
made up of a series of angled rods that support the clothing rails. It suggests an art installation — and adds to the
art gallery concept. "The vertical lines play with the horizontal angled lines of the rear casual and denim collection
walls." A wedge-shaped cash desk is integrated into this
play of lines and the mannequins along the wall add the
suggestion of movement.

Menswear is located at the rear of the right side of the
store. The shoppers pass through a screen of vertical angled rods that are backed up by a vertical, high-gloss,
grained wood wall where the garments are presented. Dis-

play tables, finished in high gloss white and grained wood
have pivoting table tops whose angles can be changed. By
changing the angle of the table top "a new dynamic for visual merchandising is accomplished." Slanted mirrors —
once again adding to the asymmetry and angular feel of
the design — and sculptured seating appears in both the
women's and men's changing rooms which are spacious,
gracious and luxurious.

"The overall effect of the store is of a simple, white art
gallery space with individual sculptured forms and a clever play of angled lines that change through the space.
Whatever position the store is viewed from there is the feel
of a constantly evolving space where the product is the art
and the visual merchandising the theater."

Burberry
Vienna, Austria

DESIGN
Gruschwitz GmbH, Munich, Germany and Moscow, Russia
Wolfgang Gruschwitz

PHOTOGRAPHY
Xaver Lockau

Located on an old pedestrian street in Vienna, in a building that is over 150 years old, is the new Burberry store as designed by Wolfgang Gruschwitz of Gruschwitz GmbH. Though the building is under the protection of the local historic society, respectful and approved additions were made to the façade that now features glass, steel, accents of gold, and LED lighting. From the street, the ground and first level are open for viewing with displays filling the many floor-to-ceiling glass display windows. Complementing the merchandise presentations are the very large lifestyle photographs that help to set the look for this new concept store.

Little remains of the "antique" interior since the walls, floors and built-in merchandise units are all new and contemporary. According to Wolfgang Gruschwitz, the client's requirements included a new glass roof, an elevator, display niches for theme-oriented merchandise presentations, the use of warm oak woods, and a rich lighting plan that would render highlights and shadows. Gruschwitz feels that he and his team met all the re-

quirements and has produced "a warm, cozy atmosphere where the customer can feel at home — on a very high level."

The interior maintains the structural qualities of the old building: a series of connecting "rooms" and a staircase that connects the street-level women's shop with the menswear on the first level. On both levels natural finishes and neutral colors are combined and oak gives a warm glow to the floors and to some of the furniture and wall units on ground level, in the women's area. On that level the oak is blended with beige carpeting and other light-colored lacquered woods.

In the women's area recessed wall spaces are self illuminated so that, not only do these niches glow, but the handbags, shoes and other accessories are all visible in full light. Gloves and scarves are used to accessorize the Burberry handbags as well as the fully outfitted headless mannequins that are on the floor showing off the new looks. Adding a nice touch to this area are the "antique" chairs that contrast with the sleek contemporary lines of the store's design.

Headless mannequins and attention getting displays invite shoppers to walk up the angled staircase to the men's department which, in contrast, is dark and dramatic. The furniture and furnishings are clean and contemporary.

In the lighting plan, the designer specified Phillips CDM-TC 35W at 4500 Kelvin for its energy saving qualities, LED in some of the display niches and 5000K all warm, XLED low voltage and PAR lamps for special areas. The overall illumination is warm and inviting — areas that glow — and dramatic shadows are created for emphasis.

In the men's department the wood is stained a very deep brown and creates strong outlines around the wall cabinets, built-ins and the display niches. According to Gruschwitz, these built-in niches resemble a gentleman's wardrobe with shelves and space for coordinated garments.

Effective visual merchandising and displays were used throughout and numerous dressed forms inhabit the space. The design team integrated them into the design and they appear as an integral element of the design just as the lighting and the fixturing was planned.

Rene Lezard

The Style Outlets, Londoner Bogen, Zweibruken, Germany

DESIGN
dan pearlman GmbH, Berlin, Germany

DECORATIVES & SHOP FITTINGS
Rene Lezard

PHOTOGRAPHER
diephotodesigner.de

The dan pearlman retail architecture firm of Berlin recognized that Rene Lezard unites individuality, modernity, style and taste, and the creative use of detail into a single brand package. The design, created for the 3,000 sq. ft. shop in The Style Outlets in Zweibruken, had to reflect all those qualities as well. Thus, the shop concept, as shown here, "conveys timelessness and a sense of well being."

Just as the Rene Lezard brand is marked by "classiness, clean forms and fine materials," so does the architectural concept for this shop carry through the message and allow the garments to shine through. To enhance the shopper's experience in a unique way there is a lounge area which has been detailed like a living room and affects a home-like ambiance. For the product presentation, the designers used hanging and front-out presentations as well as tiered tables to "loosen the look and feel" of the space. The lighting focuses on the garments and allows

them to step forward. In the lounge area the lighting is softer and gentler to create a cozier and more intimate feeling.

According to the designers the biggest challenge was "how to cope with high merchandise density (as for an outlet shop) and still create "an emotional experience." After all, the Rene Lezard name stands for up-market, designer quality garments for men and women and even here in an outlet — that level of brand recognition had to be "transferred into the shop design and without having much of a storing space." As one peruses these images of the shop, the simple white fixtures, bleached light wood floors, the blacked out industrial ceiling, area rugs and leather seating all offer suggestions of designer-class values.

Tommy Hilfiger

Fifth Ave., New York, NY

DESIGN
Callison, Seattle, WA and the **Hilfiger Creative Team**

PHOTOGRAPHY
Callison / Chris Eden

Tommy Hilfiger has made it to Fifth Avenue — in the upper 50s — where the brand has established its presence in its largest retail store worldwide. Here the retailer is rubbing display windows with shops and boutiques bearing some of the most prestigious designer names in the world. As Tommy Hilfiger said, "As an iconic thoroughfare, Fifth Avenue is the perfect home for all our collections. The Fifth Avenue store represents the mix of aspirational yet affordable — the foundation and heritage of our brand philosophy."

To meet its expectations, the company called upon Callison of Seattle to work with the Hilfiger creative team to turn the existing 22,000 sq. ft. building into an architectural representation of the Hilfiger brand. Inspired by "modern meets traditional" and based on 20th century architecture with clues from the work of McKim, Mead and White, the new Tommy Hilfiger store covers four stories and a mezzanine. A dramatic, modern staircase — centralized in the design — serves not only as a connection between the floors but also as a viewing platform for an art installation. "Designed digitally, the staircase resembles a floating sculpture that provides continuous views of Fifth Avenue — complete with Brazilian cherry treads and glass railings." Color-changing LEDs add another special touch to the staircase design.

A comprehensive Tommy Hilfiger lifestyle collection is contained in the store. The main/ground floor offers sportswear in a surround of walnut panels set off by ivory drapes — "channeling the charm of a library and men's club." The leather furnishings combined with the cherry wood floors add to the desired effect. Downstairs, on the lower level, the Hilfiger denim collection has a bar-inspired wrap desk that comes with stools. There is also a seating area "all set for comfortable lounging." Men's tailored clothing and accessories are shown on the mezzanine where the shopper can view the main level as well as the lower level from the glass railing capped with leather. The fixtures are oil rubbed bronze metal that refer back to the elegance and refinement of the now restored original Indiana limestone façade.

The second floor with its Tommy Hilfiger trademark 1960s Venini chandeliers and Brazilian cherry wood herringbone patterned floor houses women's sportswear. The women's runway collection is on the third floor and has a black lacquered floor. Glass doors open onto a balcony that overlooks Fifth Avenue In addition, the store features exclusive product offerings, upscale retail services such as a tailor, shoe shine and even iconic American snacks. There are also complimentary monthly activities such as personal denim fittings, appearances by celebrity stylists, monogramming, and even special night-time shopping hours. Throughout, the store is enriched and enhanced with artwork, antiques, artifacts and found objects that all add a distinctive look to the store. The new global packaging features shopping bags and ancillary made from 100% recycled materials.

Tommy Hilfiger is home — back where he belongs— in the city where he started 20 years ago.

James Perse

Malibu, CA

DESIGN
Marmol Radziner, Los Angeles, CA

PHOTOGRAPHY
Joe Fletcher

This is a study in contrasts. It's all black and white — inside and outside — smart and sophisticated, yet warm and welcoming. It is the new James Perse shop — a lifestyle store — located in what was formerly the timber storage warehouse of the Malibu Lumber Yard — now a sustainable, green-tinted development. As Marmol Radziner, the designer of this project, describes it — "Like James Perse clothing, the store combines modern elegance and simple luxury with the cool comfort of an ocean breeze."

That "ocean breeze" seems to sweep over the black-

stained siding of the exterior and the black-stained louvered doors that extend across the length of the shopfront. The louvers are adjustable and can be opened to allow daylight to flood the already light, white interior space. These louvered doors are also designed to pivot — to open and stack — thus opening up the entire front wall to expose the shop interior and make it one with the sheltered deck. "What results is a seamless transition between the interior of the store and the exterior deck, which serves as an informal merchandise display area and outdoor living room."

The interior — warmly lit and white — carries through the beach house concept since it is laid out like a house and divided into room-like areas; the kitchen, the living room, the dining room and the bedroom. The tall painted oak cabinetry, reclaimed oak flooring and the exposed wood ceiling add to the "beach house" ambiance. The tall display cabinets incorporate full height sliding panels that facilitate the frequent and easy changing of the visual displays. The solid sliding panels also allow for extra stock to be stored on the sales floor "out of sight but within easy reach."

White walls, white furniture and beach/nautical inspired furniture and furnishings set the look for this shop that sells the assorted James Perse designed merchandise. It is a reflection of "the quintessential Southern California lifestyle" of the designer and his work.

TSE Cashmere

Wooster Street, Soho, New York, NY

DESIGN
Janson Goldstein JJC., New York, NY

PHOTOGRAPHY
Mikikio Kikuyama Photography

The age old comfort of cashmere gets contemporary styling at TSE Cashmere. The comfort and craftsmanship of the product inspired the Janson Goldstein design firm to create this retail setting for the high end brand. The design is based on the juxtapositioning of the "quintessential Soho loft" found space with modern, luxurious finishes.

Alyson Day, VP of Marketing for TSE said, "The new store [in Soho] had to reflect the character of our knitwear product and also that of the loft space, playing on shape and texture — with a modern sensibility and clean lines. We wanted to achieve a light, airy feel, with a palette and texture that references cashmere."

The shop is located in an historic landmark building on Wooster Street where the space is long and narrow but gets wider as it extends back. Three TSE lines had to be accommodated in the space: The TSE line appears up front while the men's line and TSEasy (the contemporary line) share the back space. "Good circulation was crucial to giving the customer a sense of direction, but in a casual way that would allow them to logically flow through the store and see the complete product offering upon entry," said Steven Scuro, a partner at Janson Goldstein.

The loft space consists of existing brick walls that were sandblasted and then left in their natural state. The oak flooring that was already there was stripped, bleached and then refinished "to be lighter and brighter and harmonious with the new palette." And, though still exposed, the duct-work and piping that runs along the now white ceiling has been reorganized "to be more aesthetically resolved."

To translate the tactile quality of the product, highly lacquered wall panels — finished in a soft white — were "hung" from the walls creating a ribbon effect. The finish of these panels serves as a contrast to the brick walls and wood floors. The designers describe the panels as "fluid — with curved corners and edges. Within the panels there is a pattern of vertical gouged strips that increases and decreases in density as the space enfolds. These strips are curved in both profile and at their ends — further increasing the fluid nature of the wall. The smooth lacquered finish of these panels contrasts and complements the rich intricate textures of the cashmere fashion."

The space is fixtured simply, with a system made of softly curved, satin-finished, stainless steel bars. Some of these bars are suspended from the ceiling so that the garments seem to float in air. Others are free-standing in front of the walls thus "freeing them from the patterned panels behind — which enhances the fluidity of those panels. The lightness of the fixtures visually reinforces and brings forward the color and texture of the product."

Steven Scuro, when interviewed for an article that appeared in Contract magazine, summed it up this way, "We just opened up the space, and let it breathe — in essence transforming it back to what it always should have been."

Anthropologie
Chelsea Market, Chelsea, New York, NY

DESIGN
Pompei A.D., New York, NY
Ron Pompei

EXECUTIVE DIRECTOR OF DESIGN
Randhir Singh

The newly opened 15,000 sq. ft,, bi-level Anthropologie store in the Chelsea Market in the Chelsea area of New York City is another in a long line of unique retail spaces created for that company by Ron Pompei and the Pompei A.D. design team.

"No two Anthropologie stores are alike, and the Chelsea Market location was designed to complement not only the existing space but also the entire building and the industrial aesthetic of the surrounding neighborhood. The layout works to preserve and respect the historic value of Chelsea Market, while introducing strong visual and experiential moments to draw in visitors." Pompei A.D.'s overall design concept incorporates rich, sensual and engaging environments that integrate elements of the existing architecture into the design. "Merchandise is integrated into a variety of creative vignettes and displays designed to offer customers an entire look at a distinct lifestyle. This artful visual merchandising provides connections between store design, the merchandise and the customer. Strong word of mouth through the community is key to the store's suc-

cess, and Pompei A.D.'s designs provide a venue for that community to express themselves"

Three main areas on the first floor tie the store together: the corner entry vestibule, the main corridor entry and the staircase leading to the lower level. Each of these areas is oriented on a shifted plan from the existing shell and acts as both visual and directional cues that lead shoppers through the space. The inside surfaces of each area are covered in richly patterned concrete tiles in assorted shades of blue and white. White concrete precast treads in the angular, double-height ceiling of the staircase lead to the lower level. Custom glass illuminated globes are suspended above the stairs and they are arranged in an arched shape. This "pays homage to the existing vaulted ceiling throughout the space." Adding to the natural light that comes into the store, there are hidden overhead cove lighting on the retail floor.

There is a cluster of dressing rooms located on the lower level and they "have an outdoor market feel with distressed wood and fan shaped mosaic tile floors." In addi-

tion, the store is filled with sculptural vignettes, unique and unusual fixtures and furniture, and found objects that invite shoppers to "explore Anthropologie's 'flea-market' treasures.

Ron Pompei, the visionary head of Pompei A.D. has for some time championed the 3Cs of Retail. They are Culture, Community — and, of course, Commerce, and Pompei feels that a successful retail space should accommodate and accomplish all three in design harmony. A store should be a place to shop, learn and socialize. Following is the designer's statement with regard to this new store in a revitalized old warehouse structure on the west side of

Manhattan where the Meat Packing district and Chelsea rub up against each other.

"In total, Anthropologie creates an atmosphere of exploration and discovery that elevates customer's sense of participation and creative expression. This in turn generates more frequent visits and longer stays than traditional retail. It is an authentic and intimate landscape to be explored at length, with multiple destinations that serve as reference points in place of traditional aisles."

Levi's

Regent St., London, UK

DESIGN
Checkland Kindleysides, London

DESIGNERS
Jeff Kingsley, Joe Evans, Matt Beal, Maggie Wright

PROJECT MANAGERS
Hana Long, Karen Robertson

PHOTOGRAPHY
Keith Parry

The recently relaunched, 8,500 sq. ft. Levi's flagship store "provides Londoners and the capital's visitors a complete brand experience at the ultimate jean destination," So says the team at Checkland Kindleysides who have created numerous new looks for this renowned brand. "The store is set to both inspire and engage customers as they are taken on a journey through the origins of denim and the brand's evolution whilst offering a unique and personalized way to buy jeanswear."

Let the designers introduce the store in their own words. "The store is designed as a journey through an artisan's working environment and starts as you step off the street into a 'courtyard,' an area which is crafted to feel like an open, exhibition like space. With a whitewashed ceiling and reclaimed brick walls it provides a light and airy entrance to the store. This transition space is called 'Origin' and forms the opening 80 sq. meters of the store. The space is reserved purely for curation of craft, and is designed to create a vibrant, engaging and creative experience of the world of Levi's. 'Origin' will showcase everything from exclusive product collaboration to art exhibitions providing a level of intrigue and impact unique to fashion retailing. It serves to highlight new and innovative product whilst capturing the imagination and making a connection between youthful creativity and the workplace of the artisan, compelling visitors to explore further."

The newest fashions are on view in the main body of the store entered through two huge factory doors. "There is a clean and industrial look and feel, reflective of a workshop or factory. It's deliberately purposeful and real, meaningly designed to be robust and with function." Since this is an area that is constantly changing, the simple, functional fixtures and furniture are flexible. Though the central display fixtures are suggestive of a haberdasher's counter, they are constructed with a metal framework, Georgian wired glass panels and with a cream stove-enamel finish, to create an industrial look. Products are also displayed on metal palettes with stacked blocks "giving the feel of a factory loading bay." The palettes and blocks can be built into a range of matrices to affect tiered displays. Oak and bonded glass units are sometimes incorporated to show off the accessories. Rolling racks and shelving are used to present the folded and hung garments while — at a higher level — seasonal imagery and duck canvas frames show off the newest products. Along the left side wall, running over the stairwell, is a bridge that serves as a product gallery. "This stove enameled, metal cow paneling is inspired by textile inspection cabinets and provides a canvas where seasonal and promotional stories can be told."

Leading to the basement sales area is a modern staircase with backlit glass risers and "Levi's ZZ" laser-cut into the treads. Along the stair wall is the more than 16 ft. long

gallery wall inspired by glass fronted storage cabinet. In the basement shoppers can see a genuine vintage product display where an original 1920s 201 Jean is encased in glass and backed up by tailor's patterns. The jeans serves as a visual signpost to the adjacent Vintage Clothing Collection. The 501 Jeans Warehouse is located at the end of the 16 ft. long cash desk and it is separated from the rest of the merchandise display by floor-to-ceiling glazing and has been designed with a mirrored back wall "to give the impression of a seemingly never ending 501 Jeans vault." The most popular of the 22 different washes are presented on an easy-to-shop counter in the center.

In the Inspection Room shoppers may shop by either fit or finish. The key fits and finishes are displayed on forms in illuminated stove enameled inspection cabinets and a simple letter/number navigation system takes shoppers to where that jean is located in the adjacent wall bays.

A staircase, in the front of the basement, leads up to the fitting rooms and the stairs also serve as display risers for the Levi's footwear. The shoes are displayed on oak blocks. The fitting rooms are crafted with reproduction of duck canvas such as was used by Levi's in the 19th century. The doors are scaled down versions of the heavy, industrial doors used at the front of the store. A display of vintage weaver's shuttles "pays a subtle homage to the brand's craft and roots."

"Levi's has created a place where craftsmanship and authenticity deliver the most genuine experience of the brand in Europe," said Tim Larcombe, General Manager Levi's UK Group. "It will provide Londoners and the capital's visitors with the ultimate opportunity to engage with Levi's in a unique way."

Zara

Portal de l'Angel, Barcelona, Spain

DESIGN
Zara's Architectural Studio

PHOTOGRAPHY
Courtesy of Inditex Group

The internationally-recognized ZARA brand, that sets the fashion look for trendy young men and women, recently opened a mega flagship store in Barcelona that not only features fashion apparel and accessories but also introduces a Zara Home department. What makes this store so extra special is that it is the first retail project in Europe ever to be awarded LEED (Leadership in Energy and Environmental Design) Certification. This means that this store has met the U.S. standards for sustainable architecture and makes it the first really GREEN store in Barcelona.

The goals set by the architects/designers at Inditex, the in-house Zara designers, were to incorporate energy-efficiency and sustainability, optimize environmental management, use of water intelligently, re-use and recycled materials, and thus become an eco-efficient store. Now, at least 50 percent of the energy supply comes from renewable energy sources, the CO_2 emissions are reduced as is the consumption of electricity.

The new store at Portal de l'Angel has "an avant garde ap-

pearance of significant dimensions" and has been gently placed into "a classical landscape" says the Inditex Group. "The aim is to generate a real dialogue between diverse architectural styles, something which already occurs in the street which has buildings from very different periods. A dialogue which should serve, not to impose a certain protagonism, but to insert a new visual element which relates harmonically with an urban landscape of great quality." The façade of the store serves as a "bridge between the street, the city and the commercial space." It is a geometric composition of large squares of metal and glass and a super gigantic logo spelled out across the front — "all enveloped in light in an absolutely novel way." At street level the product displays are presented in the numerous tall glass encased windows.

The interior is a medley of off-white, grays and black rendered in a variety of textures. The merchandise is presented on five floors. Children's fashions are located in the basement while the women's collections appearing on ground level and on the first floor. Menswear is on view on the second level and the new concept, Zara Home, takes over the third floor. The centrally located escalators not only connect the assorted levels but "become a visual element of great intensity thanks to the lighting system with LEDs." Throughout the store "the lighting has been studied as an element which is clearly associated with the product, so as to permit observation without distortion and at the same time, modifying our perception of spaces and creating a special identity and atmosphere for the store." Also, rather than a straight-line traffic flow, the designers have created one that offers the shoppers more options.

Though the new store incorporates especially designed fixtures, furniture and design elements — like the graffiti painted on the walls on the second level and the Barcelona motifs in the Children's area, there are numerous pieces that have been re-used or repurposed for this green store. In addition, technologies were used throughout that ensure the least possible environmental impact from the store and the activity in the store.

In gaining the LEED Certification, the designers specified 100% recyclable stone for flooring and the surface coverings for the walls and furniture, as well as the paints, lacquers and varnishes that were used are all free of VOC (volatile organic compounds), and environmentally friendly. Recyclable materials are readily collected in specified areas in the store and cardboard boxes that the garments are delivered in to the store are collected and returned to either be reused or recycled. The paper bags are made of wood pulp derived from forests that "are exploited in a sustainable and responsible way." Even the plastic bags are biodegradable.

"This new store of the Inditex Group in Barcelona is an ambitious and innovative exercise in the matter of commercial architecture and interior decoration. Based on a profound commitment to the city and its inhabitants, we find ourselves before a space created to be enjoyed; conceived with daring but marked with respect for a town which is especially sensitive to the relation between the city, its aesthetics and its structures, and the life of its citizens."

Hickey Freeman

East Oak St. Chicago, IL

DESIGN
JGA, Southfield, MI

CHAIRMAN
Ken Nisch

CREATIVE DIRECTOR
Mike Curtis

PROJECT MANAGER
Alvin Stephenson

FOR HARTMARX CORP.
GROUP PRESIDENT, HICKEY FREEMAN
Paulette Garafolo

VP MERCHANDISING
John Morales

DIRECTOR OF RETAIL
Phil Kornblatt

DIRECTOR OF VISUAL MERCHANDISING
Robert Greco

PHOTOGRAPHY
Laszlo Regos Photography, Berkley, MI

SPACE
3,897 sq. ft.

When JGA was commissioned to design the new Hickey Freeman menswear store on East Oak Street — a major fashion venue in Chicago — the objective was to create "an American place for an American classic." Being around — fashion-wise — for more than 135 years does mean something! Surrounded on all sides by fashion icons like Hermès, Prada and the new, glowing Barneys store, the designers at JGA found their inspiration in classic American interiors and brought together heroically scaled columns, translucent glass block and limed oak casework accented with an assortment of antiques and comfortable, man-size lounge seating. "A series of levels, a legacy of the location's former residential heritage, provide segmentation and intimacy for the various product segments ranging from sportswear, furnishings, accessories and suitings."

The store's façade creates a "tailor-made" destination in its

blend of classic materials such as limestone, painted brick and the architecturally scaled moldings that accentuate doors and windows. The effectiveness of this first impression is enhanced by the 14 ft. ceiling that "adds a sense of lightness and airiness to the entry." A limestone floor adds to that impression.

The monumental stairway — just inside the entry — leads to the upper level and also serves as a stage for a cluster of dressed forms showing off some of the store's collections. These forms — in varying outfits — appear and reappear as constant companions to the shopper as he moves from "room" to "room."

According to the JGA design team, the materials used, "have the refinement, elegance and scale to complement the practical yet luxurious products." The lighting brings the neutral palette to life, highlighting the subtle textures, patterns and warmth of the fabrics.

The dark wood of the stair's risers contrast with the white woodwork and the rails. Photographs from the Hickey Freeman archives are placed on the wall along the staircase and they "celebrate the brand's American roots and unique relationship with presidents, moguls and literary luminaries."

A secondary staircase, at the rear of the ground floor, leads up to the boy's department. Here, an arched, glass block display area becomes the store's most intimate space in terms of size and height and its smaller scale complements the smaller scaled garments.

On the second level is a large suiting department with a focal circular accessory table over which hangs custom lighting fixtures. On this floor there is a lounge and custom suit area with leather club chairs and a custom Parson's style wood and leather work table, as well as a great view onto East Oak Street through the floor to ceiling windows. In other areas exposed brick walls are accented with more heritage photography.

For those who can't, or won't, walk the staircase, there is a custom designed elevator finished in bronze and wood. Since customer comfort is of prime concern at Hickey Freeman, there are richly appointed dressing rooms finished in dark mocha grass cloth and furnished with overscaled mirrors, custom light fixtures and decorative accessories. The "cultivated, affluent male who likes to dress well" will find a fitting and suit-able home at Hickey Freeman on East Oak Street.

Weiss & Goldring

Alexandria, LA

DESIGN
Michael Malone Studio @ WKMC Architects, Dallas, TX

PROJECT ARCHITECT/DESIGNER
Michael Malone, AIA

PROJECT ARCHITECT
Alesha Niedziela, Assoc. AIA

PROJECT MANAGER
Paul Pascarelli, AIA

GENERAL CONTRACTOR
Bollinger Builders, Alexandria

FIXTURE CONTRACTOR
Greg Jenkins/Cabinet Pro, Alexandria, LA

PHOTOGRAPHER
Jud Haggard

A family business that was founded well over a century ago and still a fashion institution in central Louisiana, Weiss & Goldring has relocated again and is now making a generational switch under the direction of Ted Silver. His vision of this operation, which was a broad-base upscale store for men and women, is now as a premiere men's wear retailer with a strong presence in jewelry and some special categories for women. He envisions that this new store "will put a premium on comfort and service while offering outstanding collections of high quality clothing. The goal is to support customers with a total wardrobe approach, have clothing that is accessible, but edited to reflect current styles and trends."

As designed by Michael Malone Studio of WKMC Architects of Dallas, the store is organized into two zones: an open, flexible area and a more private hospitality and fitting environment. There are two entrances to the open sales area that converge at the jewelry/accessories/scents counter. This sinuous, curved unit is also the cash/wrap desk. Four separate areas of clothing displays are set around this focal element. Each quadrant is similarly designed with hanging bins fitted with recessed standards that can accommodate hanging or shelves. Valances conceal dedicated

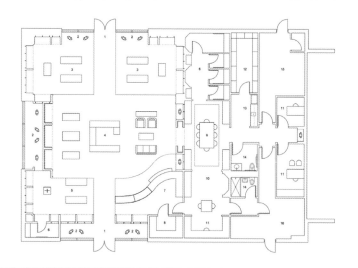

fluorescent lighting in each bin. Less flexible in its fixture design is the fifth wall, opposite the entry into the fitting section, that is set up as a shirt and match-up area.

Since an informal lunch is on the program for customers who may be coming by for a fitting or a purchase, a large family-style dining table is the heart of the hospitality/fitting area. This has become a Weiss & Goldring tradition that now finds regulars, visitors, vendors and family members gathered around the table. When not used for dining, the table serves as a lay-down/match-up table and is often covered with swatches or rolls of fabric. Off of this area is a cluster of dressing rooms and a three way mirror. There is also an executive fitting room furnished with an

informal seating area. This is part of Ted Silver's spacious office.

Michael Malone sums up his approach to the design concept. "Built using a modest budget, the store has painted gypsum board walls, acoustic tile ceilings, sealed concrete floors with carpet defining the four merchandising quadrants. Fixtures are clear finished maple plywood, mixed with classic contemporary furniture pieces and a few carefully selected antiques. Emphasis is on lighting, planning and organization — not materials and finishes — and the store becomes a back drop to excellent merchandising and impeccable service."

Destination XL

Schaumburg, IL

The "big guys" have all the luck! Not only can they see over the heads of crowds, but now they have a 12,000 sq. ft. store all to themselves. As designed by the JGA design team of Southfield, MI, the new Destination XL (DXL) in Schaumburg, IL caters to big and tall men who "seek choices in value and luxury apparel, convenience, and a more unique shopping experience for dress, casual and active attire." This is an all-inclusive, superstore concept and it reinforces the DXL brand as a leader in XL (extra large) men's fashions and accessories.

DESIGN
JGA, Southfield, MI

CHAIRMAN
Ken Nisch

CREATIVE DIRECTOR
Gordon Eason

PROJECT MANAGER
Mike McCahill

Client Team:
DIRECTOR OF STORE PLANNING
Dan Pitts

VP, VISUAL DIRECTOR OF IN-STORE BRANDING
Mark Albert

VISUAL COMMUNICATION DIRECTOR
Christina Eustace

VISUAL MERCHANDISING MANAGER
Cheri Gerzabek

PHOTOGRAPHY
Mark Steele Photography, Columbus OH

The store houses a wide range of clothing, shoes and accessories in "good, better and best" products — presented with a lifestyle focus. Not only are there private brands available, but the shopper can also select from designer brands such as Polo Ralph Lauren, Calvin Klein, Tommy Bahama, Kenneth Cole and Haan shoes. As explained by the JGA designers, "DXL provides a full lifestyle portfolio of brand, life stage, lifestyle fashion, and basic apparel choices. This breadth of assortment, consumer segmentation, and price points provide a full flavored opportunity to create a portfolio of experiences that help the customer understand this diversity, as well as this clear segmentation of product and use."

The overscaled — but proportionately BIG atrium window on the exterior offers a drawing point to shoppers in the heavily trafficked area. "The bold use of the brand's iconic colors, forms and iconography form the DXL mark, and the dark bronze portal entry, the graphic nature of the awnings

are eye-catching on a drive-by basis, yet intimate and welcoming at a pedestrian level." Inside the store, the shopper's eye takes over and quickly is directed by quality cues, visual runways and the effective presentation of key items. The assorted departments are distinctive in finishes, tone and feel, still the design team has created a sense of "continuity, consistency and a familiarity for the guest." Runways and large elevated platforms define the store's key action zones such as active, studio, club and casual. Each zone or department features mannequins, props, and feature lighting. While the mannequins in the studio area are more casual and relaxed in attitude, the ones in club are more reserved and formal in pose and appearance.

Porcelain tile floors have been laid throughout to "create a consistent upscale look" while the area rugs that are set atop the tiles define the various zones in the store. The active zone is highlighted by action-posed mannequins on a runway with a multisport technical finish. The zone's focal

wall suggests a skybox view through its stadium-like architecture and is complemented by the backlit illuminated graphics. A denim bar is highlighted in the studio area. It is constructed of end block rustic timber on a raw steel base. Here, the runway has a raw welded steel frame topped with sheets of diamond-stamped metal. The runway is accentuated by the vintage bulb and cast glass decorative lighting. The graphic T-shirt focal element is framed by the stock shelving wall fixtures and in keeping with the loft-like ambience, there is a secondary ceiling of suspended timbers. The vintage pool table serves as a lay-down display area — or can actually be used to be played upon.

The leather topped runway, the striped accent carpet and the nickel and walnut fixtures create the casual dress zone. This area is adjacent to the shoe department which has a puck wall system and underlet feature tables, "making it an

ideal product bridge between the store's more casual and sophisticated dress areas." Tailored clothing is housed in club where nickel and wenge wood fixtures are used along with a backlit illuminated outrigger system. An exotic wood covers the top of the club's runway.

The essentials zone appears at the store's hub with major impact walls for stocking key items on its perimeter. The fitting rooms are located here and set into a curved wall. Each fitting room is accented with a perimeter mega graphic with images of masculine objects or activities. "Quality cues such as custom millwork, environmentally friendly flooring material, and upgraded lighting are an unexpected and welcome amenity in an unexpected place." It looks like the big and large boys do have all the luck!

Urban Outfitters

East 86th St., New York, NY

DESIGN
Pompei A.D., New York, NY

CREATIVE DIRECTOR & PRINCIPAL
Ron Pompei

EXECUTIVE DIRECTOR OF DESIGN
Randhir Singh

At Urban Outfitters you always expect the unexpected. You expect something unique and different. Somehow they always find new ways to use old things — to reuse, repurpose, reclaim and rehab — even when the space is new.

The two-level store — designed by Pompei AD of New York City, a firm that has created numerous unusual and memorable spaces for Urban Outfitters — fills a 12,000 sq. ft. space in a new condominium building on East 86th Street in Manhattan. Ron Pompei, the Creative Director and Principal of Pompei A.D. explains, "We have worked with Urban Outfitters for over 20 years to develop and evolve their retail strategy. Each store we have completed for the company employs a site-specific design that preserves the original character of the space and responds to the distinct physical and cultural context of its location."

The "statement" begins on the storefront which includes a helter-skelter arrangement of strips of wood over the doorway that is recessed into the existing limestone facade. The steel plate signage runs around the rectangular opening like a proscenium and also frames the display windows. Throughout the two-level shop the motif, introduced over the store's entrance, appears and reappears. As Randhir Singh, Executive Director of Design at Pompei A.D. said, "Working within a concrete shell, we were able to offset this basic material by infusing the floors and walls with explosive patterns of wood planks. The fitting

room and stairway design picks up the use of wood and forms a sculptural landscape within the space. The result is a warm and inviting experience that stays current and edgy for the customer."

Throughout there is a natural, unfinished, and urban look to the space. In addition to the pattern of the climbing and tumbling wood through the space and across the raw walls, the exposed ceilings filled with pipes and ducts and the natural wood floors add to the overall feel of the shop. The criss-crossed motif is even impressed into the concrete block that serves as the cash/wrap. Light, natural wood slabs of wood serve as the shelves and as the tops of some tables that have vintage metal legs or use old sewing machine bases as supports. Complementing the flow of the criss-cross timber is the unusual cascading "sculpture" of all sorts of things that create a movement of their own as a focal element up front over a table lined with books. The unusual table —an antique painted wood base with a slick contemporary top — can be seen through the display window that also carries the imprint of the wood slat motif.

The space remains highly industrial and raw with areas of cinder block juxtaposed with reclaimed planks of wood and throughout the red painted pipes snake through the ceiling and walls as a strong accent. It is a space that will be remembered.

Joe Fresh

Granville St., Vancouver, BC, Canada

DESIGN
Burdifilek, Toronto, ON

CREATIVE PARTNER
Diego Burdi

MANAGING PARTNER
Paul Filek

PROJECT MANAGER
Lisa Lee

SENIOR DESIGNER
Spencer Lui

DESIGNERS
**William Lau, Helen Chen,
Samer Shaath, Jacky Kwong Cadd**

PRODUCTION
Thomas Moore, Anna Nomerovsky

PROJECT MANAGER
Tom Yip

PHOTOGRAPHY
Ben Rahn, A-Frame

Joe Fresh

Granville St., Vancouver, BC, Canada

Joe Fresh is the brand of a "home-grown, fast-fashion" retailer, and for the design of the Loblaw Company's first stand-alone Joe Fresh shop on Granville Street in Vancouver, they called upon the Toronto-based Burdifilk design firm. The concept behind the store was "to broaden the retailer's reach and to further appeal to urban shoppers." Up until the opening of this store the Joe Fresh line, which features everything from chic footwear to outdoor fashions and well-priced beauty products, was available in the Loblaw Markets where consumers could shop fashion along with their food, health and home supplies.

Large windows on the two levels of the 12,000 sq. ft. store are bisected by a sleek, horizontal canopy on the store's façade. According to the Burdifilek designers "the beautiful volume expressed in an architectural white envelop is anchored in classic simplicity — drawing from modern influences." As Diego Burdi, the creative partner of the design firm said, "We wanted to create a signature environment that was truly unique to the brand — while staying true to their fresh, modern, youthful image."

Moving from the modern white cube-like façade and the traditional buildings that surround it, into the cool, spacious and light interior, it is obvious that the designers' intent was to create a background for the collection. Color-filled women's' sportswear and accessories are on the ground level of the shop, while men's fashions has to share the upper level with women's active, sleep and lingerie products. Areas are highlighted with giant graphics, adding bold areas of color to the white walls. "This concept embraces the brand identity and provides a platform that elevates and reflects the current advertising campaign.

It's a white-on-white story! The walls, ceiling and fixture finishes are a unified palette of crisp whites, clear sandblasted acrylics, all complemented by the heavily-tex-tured, natural oak and the soft matte gray floor. The collections of brightly colored garments are either hung or stacked on a powder coated white metal wall system or tantalizingly arranged on the white finished, oversized Parsons tables that make strong horizontal statements. "The clothes themselves become the focal point and inject an ever-changing spectrum of color to the environment."

Joe Fresh offers Canadians stylish, fresh and affordable apparel and accessories and is the Loblaw Company's answer to consumers for accessible, of-the-moment style. Already roll outs of this design are appearing in Canada in Mississauga, Brampton, and Vaughn, Ontario, as well as in Alberta and soon to appear in Toronto.

American Eagle Outfitters

Times Square, New York, NY

DESIGN ARCHITECT
BAR Architects, San Francisco, CA with
American Eagle's In-House Team

BAR ARCHITECTS TEAM:
PARTNER IN CHARGE
Susan McComb

DESIGN LEADER
David Schwing

PROJECT DESIGNER
Johannes Pareigis

AMERICAN EAGLE IN-HOUSE TEAM:
VP CONSTRUCTION
John Bezek

VP MARKETING
Keith Kaplan

DIRECTOR STORE DESIGN
Michael Smith

SENIOR MANAGER STORE DESIGN
Mat Sabella

SENIOR MANAGER FIXTURE DESIGN
Mark Wolff

SUPERVISOR PROJECT DESIGN
Ken Nanna

PROJECT MANAGER CONSTRUCTION
J.P.Morabito

ARCHITECT OF RECORD
Alan Gaynor & Co. PC, NYC

PHOTOGRAPHY
Adrian Wilson and Courtesy of American Eagle

It's all *entertainment!* Along with theatres, movie houses, dining and dancing and people-watching — shopping must rank up there high in what entertainment is all about. So, if business is about "location, location, location," what could be a more appropriate space for a youth oriented casual/active wear company than on Times Square — *the entertainment* district of New York City — where day into evening and most of the night, the area is filled with throngs of young, fun-loving, mall-going *habitué's* from around the country and the world. Times Square is turning into a sort of outdoor mall and now located across from the TKTS booth where literally hundreds line up daily for discounted theater

tickets, is the new four story, 30,000 sq. ft. American Eagle store designed by BAR Architects of San Francisco. BAR was commissioned "to transform a nondescript speculative building into a functional, high performing flagship that would represent the American Eagle (AE) brand" This new space provided an opportunity to refresh AE's overall store design with the quintessential urban feeling of Times Square.

As anticipated by AE and the BAR design team, there is always a volume of shoppers in the store and the expanded entry on the corner and the upgraded interior circulation accommodate the heavy traffic. The four floors have been turned into "a series of vibrant and interconnected retail

spaces" that are connected by an ornamental iron staircase, escalators and a bank of elevators. According to the design team, "each floor was conceived as a unique shopping environment to encourage exploration throughout the building."

Michael Smith, American Eagle's director of store design and his team worked closely with David Schwing and the BAR group to "establish the tone and personality of the store design." That included the choice of materials and colors as well as the customized store elements such as the mezzanine "to maximize the efficiency of the tight footprint to meet sales projection goals." In keeping with the store's location and its setting amid Times Square's lights, glitz, glitter and frenetic visual activity, the Barnycz Group of Baltimore was

called upon to create the 15,000 sq. ft of LED screens that cover the store's façade and, for 18 hours each day, burst forth in full color to claim AE's stake on the scene.

The LED screens continue inside the store where they greet shoppers before the fashion-hungry take off, via the adjacent escalators, to the floors of their choice. The men's' floor is on the lower level where white glossy subway tiles cover the walls and girder-like elements, painted a dark color, add to the texture-rich setting that includes hickory woodwork. Denims are featured on the entry level where polished concrete is contrasted with specially designed Bocci lighting fixtures.

White fixtures and pale gray ceilings provide a softer and gentler look on the second floor where women's wear is featured. The polished concrete floors are interrupted by areas of oak for contrast and emphasis. A glass and steel wall with wood accents adds depth and dimension to the merchandise presentation. The aerie f.i.t. and dorm wear, as well as lingerie, are located on the third floor where whitewashed woods and trim create the desired ambiance.

A gallery hall is the focal spot here with its louvered panels and the whitewashed casework that lines the tall space. There is a beauty area off the gallery which has long, fixed white shelves to showcase the variety of scents on offer. The f.i.t. active wear area, on this level, is defined by its sleek fixtures and glowing walls.

Electronic media and honest materials combine along with all that theatrical jazz to attract, engage and satisfy American Eagle's youthful client base.

77Kids

Cherry Hill, NJ

DESIGN
Michael Neumann Architects (MNA), New York, NY

PRINCIPAL
Michael Neumann

PROJECT MANAGER
Vivian Prunner

DESIGN TEAM
Talin Rudy, Christine Longcore, Patrick Gegen
Benjamin Keiser

FOR AMERICAN EAGLE OUTFITTERS
PROJECT DESIGN
Michael Smith, Director, Store Design & Fixturing

STORE FIXTURING
Mark Wolff, Sr. Manager, Fixturing

STORE DESIGN & VISUAL CONSULTANT
Chele McKee

MARKETING & TECHNOLOGY
Brian Franks, VP Marketing

TECHNOLOGY CONSULTANT
RGA

GENERAL CONTRACTOR
Tom Rectenwald Construction, Harmony, PA

PHOTOGRAPHY
Jairo Camelo

American Eagle Outfitters have already secured a solid beachhead in the teens-to-twenties market and now, in an effort to make inroads with their new brand for children, 77Kids, they have called upon Michael Neumann Architects of NY for this prototype design.

The store, located in Cherry Hill, NJ, is easily identified by the 77Kids signage made of found dimensional metal letters applied to a steel clad panel. The storefront is almost all glass and it is framed with white-washed plank walls and a canopy. Painted wooden signs are linked together and are reminiscent of the ice cream flavor signs in old-fashioned soda shops. According to the designers, this "sturdy, kid-friendly design seeks to promote curiosity and creativity in the customers."

Inside the 5400 sq. ft. shop, the black painted ceiling effectively lowers the height and brings the shopper's eye to the child scale fixtures set on the light, maple wood floors. The perimeter walls are clad with white-washed wood planks that add to the open and clean studio look of the space. "Whimsical and flexible, the 'building block' components (of the fixtures) are completely adaptable for fold, hang or adjustable bin drawers for smaller items." A playfully stacked "denim canyon" — centrally located — creates an impactful display for the selection of denim

styles and finishes. It also serves as an interactive space for the young shoppers where they can find fun accessories, key apparel and even the latest videos that might interest them.

The specially designed fitting rooms address the children's love for creating their own spaces. Thus, MNA's designers have created an amusing variation on the "secret forts" that children will often fashion in their game-playing. While the boy's fitting room has an in-your-face "keep out" sign, the girl's area has "peace signs" that serve as peek-a-boo porthole windows "for keeping a look-out." The inspiration for the design of the cash/wrap—and in the same playful mood — is an old fashioned ice-cream parlor counter. Here the shopper will also find "treats for personalization and gifties."

A selection of the white washed poplar, plywood, galvanized steel, white lacquer, industrial felt and natural canvas complete the design. The total design, plus the sense of comfort and fun, allows the shop to be readily appreciated and enjoyed by child and parent alike. Also — with the flexible and easily convertible fixtures, the design can be made to work in almost any space.

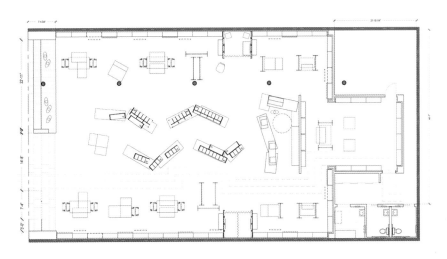

LittleMissMatched

Downtown Disney, Anaheim, CA

DESIGN
JGA, Southfield, MI

CHAIRMAN
Ken Nisch

PROJECT MANAGER
Mike McCahill

BRAND CONSULTANT
Adrienne Weiss Corp., Chicago, IL

Client Team:
CEO & CO-FOUNDER
Jonah Staw

PRESIDENT
Ann Acierno

CFO
Brigid Foster

DIRECTOR OF STORES
Rodney Hutton

PHOTOGRAPHY
Laszlo Regos Photography, Berkley, MI

Designed by JGA of Southfield, MI for "tween girls and those who are equally young at heart from ages 1 through 101," the new store for LittleMissMatched creates a brand environment that reflects a lifestyle of "fashionable fun, creativity, individuality and innovation." This is the store where shoppers find whimsical fashion accessories and lifestyle products such as flip-flops, sleepwear, bedding, and more — though it is the company's signature product — socks that don't match — sold in odd numbers, that inspires "creativity through mixing and matching."

The 1017 sq. ft. store in Anaheim is the prototype design for the brand rollout. As designed by the JGA design firm, "the store reflects a 'conceal and reveal' perspective — a peek-a-boo look at patterns reflected in mirrors and finishes that reveal that everything is not evident at first glance." Shoppers enter through "color patterned light projected on the entry floor." Hats, socks, gloves and other seasonal merchandise are displayed in the front window on dimensional dowels and spanner racks — up-lit from a white terrazzo floor element. Once inside, the store is revealed through a series of shapes and forms. There is the "Mixing Bowl" — a meeting space and the "Socks Trough" where the newest designs are presented on try-on forms and ready for mixing or matching. The clothing bays are divided by wall fixtures into merchandise alcoves. White

display panels appear on the Sock Tower and the curved feature wall that extends from floor to ceiling. "The column that extends from the merchandise towards the ceiling tempts the shoppers to explore the colorful mismatching options. There is a large circular cut-out in the wedge ceiling for the Mixing Bowl to extend through which adds to the sense of scale." Below the Mixing Bowl are bunkers that contain postcards and coloring station materials.

Layering over the front windows and the interior mirror surfaces are logos made of Lumisty glass transparent decorative film that appear and disappear as the viewing angle changes. Shapes of hearts, stars and circles are cut into the floor to reflect some of the typical patterns found on the merchandise offer. Throughout there are overscaled graphics that "encourage celebration of the brand through mismatching." They also define the fitting room area which

is located near the mailbox where shoppers can deposit their postcards.

According to the design team, "the floor plan creates a pinball effect between the merchandise elements (Mixing Bowl, Sock Trough, cash/wrap and fitting rooms)" and the cash/wrap places the customer and the sales associate side by side at the round customer transaction surfaces. Jonah Staw, CEO and Co-Founder of LittleMissMatched, said, "The packaging on our products opens like a book to tell a story of our brand. And we always direct shoppers to our site so they can play games and interact with the brand. In the store we do quirky fun, and memorable things to reinforce the brand." The new store design fulfills the promise that the brand extends.

Tiffany & Co.

Huai Hai Road, Shanghai, China

DESIGN
S. Russel Groves (SRG), New York, NY
in collaboration with **Tiffany & Co.'s
Architecture & Design group**

PHOTOGRAPHY
Courtesy of S. Russel Groves

This new Tiffany & Co. store on Huai Hai Road opened in time to coincide with the 2010 World Expo in Shanghai. As designed by the New York City based designer S. Russel Groves, working in collaboration with Tiffany's architecture and design team, "this symbol of American luxury and design extended the American presence beyond the grounds of the Expo itself."

Explaining his concept, S. Russel Groves said, "Tiffany is one of the most iconic American brands, so we wanted to strike a perfect balance between creating something that felt classic, while also making the environment feel more modern and relevant. Our design had to support the brand in very subliminal and subtle ways — without ever overwhelming it — while still moving it forward." The shop was constructed in two phases and the final stage was the store façade which had Tiffany's "blue box" as its inspiration. The exterior face consists on an upper and a lower element — "two discrete but complementary parts — to create a sense of excitement and recognition in this busy retail area." The upper area (the third to fifth floors) is covered with translucent layers of shimmering pale blue glass to create a serene yet active presence on the street. The LED infrastructure is used to create unique visual effects on this "ephemeral veil." The lower level consists of both clear and opaque bronze doors and the lower face of the building is sheathed in patterned screens. These are panels of light bronze and nickel lattice which affords shoppers on the street a glimpse into the shop. "The overall

effect of the façade is an illusion to jewelry; the screens are the filigree or metal banding support, and the blue glass is the sparkling gem."

As for the interior, Groves concept is a lighter and more feminine interpretation of Tiffany's illustrious history. A focal element is the graceful, arching stairway of marble, walnut and glass that soars through the space connecting the three levels of the shop. As it ascends from ground level to the mezzanine level it circles the crystal glass chandelier that is suspended from above. Glass fluting, silver leaf, limed oak and lacquered panels are used on the interior. Some of the surfaces that are fabricated of glass are further enriched through innovative methods of traditional artisan techniques such as eglomise, silver leafing and etching on glass.

New and exciting display techniques are used in innovative ways to tantalize the shoppers in the store. All in all, Groves design in collaboration with the Tiffany store planning and design team has created a dynamic selling experience "that imbues the rich craftsmanship and quality of the brand with 21st century technology."

Swarovski
Times Square, New York, NY

DESIGN
Tokujin Yoshioka, Tokyo, Japan

PHOTOGRAPHY
Courtesy of Swarovski

Making its shimmering and crystal clear appearance amid the noise, blitz and glitz and colorful clamor of Times Square is the new outpost for the Swarovski line of fashion jewelry and watches. The design concept —Crystal Forest — was originally designed by Tokujin Yoshioka and it was introduced in Tokyo's Ginza district a few years ago. It was soon followed by a Crystal Forest in Chicago and several other places, and now appears in New York.

Kevin Coen, Executive VP of Swarovski North America Limited's Consumer Goods Business said, "Swarovski's Crystal Forest retail design concept creates an environment that accentuates the beauty and fine craftsmanship of our product offering." He added that the setting, "creates a consumer experience that embodies Swarovski's brand value of innovation and modernity."

White lacquer and mirror stainless steel finishes pre-dominate in the relatively small shop. Textured walls feature reflective white prisms that "envelop the space to create the illusions of an organic crystal forest." The merchandise is presented in a combination of vertical and horizontal showcases that contain LED lighting coming from assorted directions. This play of light on the different materials and finishes "enhances the sparkle of the store." The floating display boxes in the open-back windows "allow for unique, eye-catching displays of Swarovski's crystal accessories" as well as a look into the shop.

This boutique joins the more than 1700 Swarovski boutiques in 120 countries. It is also an oasis of calm and tranquility in the mad scurrying of Times Square.

Wynn & Company

Wynn Hotel, Las Vegas, NV

DESIGN
David Ling Architect, New York, NY

ARCHITECT/DESIGNER
David Ling

PHOTOGRAPHY
Eric Laignel, New York, NY

Located in the deluxe Wynn Hotel in Las Vegas is Wynn & Company, a watch store designed by David Ling Architect of New York City. The design invites the shopper to step inside a watch and become part of the time and the time keeping process.

The bowed, gold-framed window is surrounded by a façade sheathed in spider marble and shaped to suggest the cylinder-shaped shop inside. Three round openings or oculi — cut into the marble surface — serve as display showcases for some of the Wynn collection of fine time pieces. Inside, the space is dominated by a giant, all-enveloping clock face on the ceiling. It's a functioning clock with hour and minute hands set to Las Vegas time (which in itself is unique since one rarely sees clocks in Vegas, the city where time stands still). The surrounding gold colored walls are over lined with nickel coil drapery that "reminds one of metal watchbands." The passing of time is marked in four distinct types of "glowing displays." A three quarter crescent shaped glass display, in the center of the space, serves as the main pivot for the shop layout "which spins around metaphysically just as a watch hand spins literally." Expanding out from this focal unit are the free-standing cylindrical vitrines or museum cases followed by the rectangular glass merchandise displayers engaged into the walls. The final display layers are the fully recessed

niches in the walls — between the rectangular vitrines. These niches "form a lyrical horizontal movement in contrast to the floor vitrines."

Contrasting with the shimmering metallic coated walls is the floor of French limestone. Though the overhead clock sets the theme and layout of the space, Ling provided a private viewing niche for "a more discreet viewing experience." The lighting plan combines indirect lighting in the walls and ceiling coves at the perimeter of the watch face which causes it to appear to float above. Adjunct display fixtures are not only self illuminated, but they receive extra light from the grouped lights that form the hour markings in the ceiling clock face.

Carlo Pazolini

Milan, Italy

DESIGN
Giorgio Borruso Design, Marina del Rey, CA

PHOTOGRAPHY
Alberto Ferrero

The multi-award winning Carlo Pazolini store in Milan has garnered almost as many awards, citations and medals as it has shoes to offer. The shop has been recognized for its architecture and design, and for its clever fixtures and innovations. Recently, it was announced that the shop and its designer, noted architect/designer, Giorgio Borruso Design, was awarded the 2011 International Architecture Award presented by The Chicago Athenaeum: Museum of Architecture and Design, and The European Centre for Architecture Art Design and Urban Studies.

The shop of about 4,000 sq. ft. is stocked with men's, women's and children's shoes and is prominently on display in the Piazza Cordusio. It is the first western European stand-alone shop for the company and this design redefines their retail concept. Since designer Giorgio Borruso is the winner of even more design awards than can be enumerated — and since he writes so eloquently about his design concepts — we are leaving it to him to explain his design concept:

"There is an ambiguous distinction between our bodies and the things we wear. Like the buildings we inhabit, we shape our clothing and it shapes us. Attempts at accu-

rately sculpting the shape of the human foot in Egyptian, classical and contemporary art imply that footwear literally shapes our feet over time. Nineteenth-century artists who wanted to recreate classical styles and complained that the feet of contemporary shoe-wearing models had to be abstracted to more closely match the feet of sandal-wearing Greek and/or Roman people. Feet contain a quarter of the body's bones — each one part of a flexible, adaptive network; each node offering the potential for that network to be subtly reshaped. As newborns, our toes quickly take on the shape of the shoes we wear, but for a brief time they are remarkably dexterous, like plaster ready to be cast by muscle memory.

"With this in mind, we used the shape of a newborn's foot as a kind of iconic 'cell' in an emergent network of display shelving and seating. Swarm Intelligence algorithms or "Swarm Predictions" are used (and sometimes ignored) to forecast problems in complex systems. In this case, the project site's proximity to the banking district was noted. Swarm Intelligence is perhaps most clearly modeled in the natural world; insect swarms, schools of fish, flocks of birds, etc. illustrate the formation of loose cellular structures that negotiate an ephemeral distinction between object and space.

"The project plays out over time, on an urban stage for the piazza, or as color compositions shift as one moves through the space. Cells also trace out their paths over time, and from larger, semi-ordered compositions. These paths manifest as metal tubing or dashed wood slat wall panels. The cellular shelving system peels away from a plaster wall, while both are reshaped by existing cast-iron columns. The plaster wall remains like a molded remnant of this activity; an over-scaled cast of some unknown sculptural detail reminiscent of the Platonic human form. The new installations wrap into each other, but, also through the historical found conditions, each shapes the other, just as our bodies both reshape and are shaped by the things we wear.

"Reinforcing this synthesis of old and new, natural and technological, the shelving and seating cells use on innovative and glue-less molding process, which bonds natural wool felt (one of the most ancient materials) with the polymer at a molecular level, thus forming a new structural composite."

Tashi
Mumbai, India

DESIGN
JGA, Southfield, MI

CHAIRMAN
Ken Nisch

CREATIVE DIRECTOR
Gordon Eason

ARCHITECT/PROJECT MANAGER
FRDC, Bangalore, India

CHIEF ARCHITECT
Sanjay Agarwal with Vineeth, Aditi, Jim, Karthika, Prachi, Shameem, Abhilash, Fazal, Sanjay

LEED CERTIFICATION/ENERGY CONSULTANT
Ms. Prerna Dhapola, Archipedition, Bangalore, India

VM PLANNING & DESIGN
Charles Perez, ADIG Studio, Concord CA

BRAND & LOGO DESIGN
Leo Burnett, Big Apple A, Mumbai, India

CLIENT TEAM
MANAGING DIRECTOR
Noel N. Tata

VP RETAIL
Deepak Deshpande

The goal set for Tashi by Tata International was to have a brand prototype shop that would combine the consumers' love of shoes and fashion with the corporation's desire for social responsibility and "green" practices. The designers at JGA had the task of designing this 3,000 sq. ft. shop in Mumbai that would show shoes for the entire family as well as leather goods such as wallets, belts and jackets. The product offering — high fashion and formal to casual and ethnic — was to be shown in a unique setting that was eco-friendly. With the assistance of FRDC, Bangalore-based architects for project management, and with the talents of Ms. Prerna Dhapola of Archiperdition to guide the design to LEED certification, the design evolved.

"For the love of shoes" became the guiding mantra or the focus along with "value and bringing together the emotion, place with product — all in an earth-friendly environment." The overscaled shoe, on the façade, immediately sets this store apart from its surrounding retailers and also serves to attract shoppers, as it makes a strong fashion statement. The oversized stiletto sculpture stands seven feet tall with a 50-inch heel and is 11 feet from back to toe. The logo is the symbol for Tashi which means "prosperity and well-being" and is represented by three dots. The dots signify "trust, reliability, service" — the three key attributes of the parent company, Tashi International.

The shop interior is zoned for men and women and within each area it is further defined by lifestyles such as City Lights, Glitz & Glam and Caravan. The women's area has curved, light and airy fixtures, pedestal tables, white finishes and butter-tone leather. "Combined with hot pink stools, it is feminine without being frilly."

More structured and block-like fixtures appear in the men's area — organized on a grid — neutral in finish with wood, taupe leather and stone. For the children's and sports sections the fixtures have radius finish and are more geometric in shape. Elements vary from small, detail-driven signage to highly communicative visuals and graphics, to tables, coasters and lampshades. The use of wood and stone wall cladding and acrylic and brushed steel distinguish everyday wear from premium. "Dynamic graphics and resourced artifacts add to the experience that brings style to life. Lighting adds sparkle, illuminates, directs, highlights and defines the merchandise and adds to the experience." For the LEED certification efforts were made to reuse existing materials and minimize imports. Leather waste from shoe manufacturing was used to finish some of the walls.

"Tashi is all about democratizing style, celebrating life to add a soul to every sole to create an ongoing lifestyle experience in-store."

Nine West

Fifth Avenue, New York, NY

DESIGN
Jones In-House Design Team

CREATIVE DIRECTOR, NINE WEST
Fred Allard

PHOTOGRAPHY
Courtesy of Nine West

With the opening of the remodeled Fifth Avenue flagship, Nine West entered into a new age and developed a new way of visually communicating the essence of the women's shoes brand. The renovation of this store, that opened in 1984, is part of the company's initiative to enhance its vertical retail operations.

Fred Allard, the Creative Director at Nine West said, "The goal was to style fashion footwear as an artwork to admire and crave. The new store milieu carries the shopper's imagination from the fashion runway to visually stimulating tables that appear to float on the tile floor. The

product is also spotlighted and illuminated with light that allows true color expression to pop and embrace all of her senses, especially through the featured artwork created by New York artist Franck Salzwedel. I believe that women see shoes as 'eye-candy' that needs to be presented to them as sculptures just waiting for the perfect admirer to fall in love with every angle."

The 2155 sq. ft. store is filled with visually stimulating fixtures and eye-arresting elements, "creating a new and intoxicating environment for shoppers." Stacy Lastrina, Executive VP of Marketing and Creative Services adds that there is what appears to be a runway in the center of the shop and the recessed black tracks in the ceiling cove further enhances that runway design. "Presentation on the perimeter walls is a stage of shoes with white risers, and thick Plexiglas shelves highlighting the product. Oversized, polished stainless steel framed mirrors divide the linear walls, drawing the shopper to the display." The use of metal halide lamps throughout is "artistically stimulating" and also energy efficient. The crisp white light allows the true color of the shoes, handbags and accessories to emerge.

Seating is integrated into the mid-floor display table fixtures and the dark gray upholstery contrasts with the sleek white finish of the tables. It also recalls the dark vertical stripes that accentuate the linear presentation of shoe styles near the entrance.

Sheryl Bloom, President of Fashion Footwear sums it up: "The design [of this store] evokes the passion that women have for shoes, and creates a shoe lover's dream. The elements and techniques used throughout the store up the ante on styling fashion footwear and make it an artwork to crave."

Hirshleifer Shoes

Manhasset, Long Island, NY

DESIGN
Sergio Mannino Studio, Brooklyn, NY
Sergio Mannino, Garnet Spagrud
Francesco Bruni, Francesca Scalatteris

GENERAL CONTRACTOR
CDS Mestel Construction

LIGHTING DESIGN
Lido Lighting, Bill Pierro Jr.

NEON SCULPTURE
Patrick Nash, Sergio Mannino

PHOTOGRAPHY
Massimiliano Bolzinella, New York, NY
max@bi-photograhy.com

Sometimes, the architect/designer becomes so lyrical and poetic in describing the space he or she has designed that the only way to do justice to the project is to let the creator speak for himself. This shoe store, designed for Hirshleifer in Manhasset NY, as the designer Sergio Mannino describes it is, "a subtle reference and an homage to the world of art and design history — mainly Italian and American."

And so, in the designer's own words: "It is indeed a space where references and memories happen in a metaphysical way and are not entirely visible at first sight — a place for dialogue between two opposite texts: the first is minimalist, rigorous and precise, alluding to the art of several American figures such as Sol LeWitt, Carl Andre or Donald Judd in its physicality and spirituality; the second is a reference to the rich, sensual, decadent, unpredictable and free world of the Radical Design groups that changed the course of design in Italy from the late '60s to the '80s.

"Space and timing are experienced through a proscenium of subtle humor and strict precision. The rigorous

formalism of the minimalists is changed by 'folies' — unexpected elements winking at you from some other world: a glass case sitting on a sofa (a reference to a 1967 piece by Italian architect Gio Ponti); a neon sculpture gently curved but burning in white artificial light (another reference to Lucio Fontana's Concetti Spaziali of the 1960s); a bloody red wall that sets the backdrop of the scene.

"As in theater nothing in the store is real or natural: the floor has wood grain but is made of ceramic tiles; the Fjord red stones by Moroso are soft and upholstered in fabric and leather; the biomorphic and the geometric shapes in the space are embedded in heavy, shiny lacquers or neon lighting, yet the result is noisy silence — indeed a statement."

Sergio Mannino and his co-designers negotiated between the styles and sources of inspiration to create an attractive shoe store with a definite look and feel. They have created a surprising space that contains a sense of continuity in spite of the contradictions in the inspiration.

Via Venetto

Glorietta 5 Mall, Makati City,
Manila, Philippines

DESIGN
Buensalido Architects, Manila, Philippines

DESIGN & PHOTOGRAPHY
Jason Buensalido

This small shop of just over 600 sq. ft. is located in the Glorietta 5 Mall in Makati City, Manila and was designed by Jason Buensalido of Buensalido Architects of Manila. According to the designer, the inspiration for this unique, exciting and involving design comes from a translation of the name. "Via" is the Italian word for roadway, walkway or path and that suggests movement — action. That, Buensalido has interpreted with this series of sharply angled and undulating arches, and the arches are connected

into an arcade by the series of beams "forming a web-like structure with folds and facets. The interior surfaces of the shop resemble a diamond which is what the brand is, 'a diamond in the rough,' a gem that is meant to sparkle in the midst of hundreds of other shoe brands."

In the blacked out space these white twisting and turning shapes are interrupted by lights woven into the arches. The whole shop is open for viewing and at the far end is a broken, angular block form that is the cash/wrap desk. Adding to the angular quality of the design are the bright, lipstick red molded plastic benches that are lined down the center of the space. Glass shelves fill in the openings between the arches and the stock is presented on them.

According to Jason Buensalido, the Philippine market reflects the up-scaling taste of the new Filipino shopper who expects more than just a better product. They are expecting good value but are also looking for more in the settings and atmosphere of the shops they patronize. The days of basic retail design are now over and the Filipino shopper anticipates a more fun shopping experience and looks forward to new, unique and creative shop design. The more up-scale the brand, the more the shopper expects from the setting. This new Via Venetto concept is attracting the attention of these discerning shoppers.

In this issue of RDI we also introduce a new toy store concept, Toy Kingdom, that is also in Manila and further evidence of the good store design and merchandise presentation being created in the Philippines.

Brundl

Kaprun, Austria

DESIGN
Blocher Blocher Partners, Stuttgart, Germany

SHOP CONSTRUCTION
Umdasch Shop Concepts GmbH, Amstetten, Austria

PHOTOGRAPHY
Courtesy of Blocher Blocher Partners

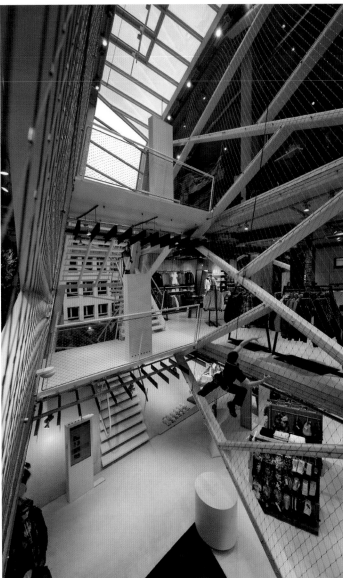

According to the designers at Blocher Blocher, the Stuttgart-based architectural firm, for the owner of the new Brundl retail store, Christoph Brundl, it is all about identity and corporate structure. His customers are people who want to leave everyday life behind for a while and find a respite. It was his desire to not only link shopping and adventure, but to create a place for communication. Thus, in the tourist town of Kaprun in Austria, the architects at Blocher Blocher Partners designed this unique retail structure that is "a landmark putting an exclamation mark at the unique business concept." The store provides skiers, hikers and outdoor lovers with all their needs and fulfills all their desires.

In the words of the designers: "There is, in the middle of the Alpine idyll, rather an object than a building. No visible stories. An edgy entity. Bizarre peaks erect into the sky. Metal lamellae vs. turned wood railings. Behind the gray hull you find a retail shop different from others. Retail is permanent pursuit of contact and dialogue. Insofar this wedge is something playful. A shift on one's perspective shifts the entire image. Now the perforated sheets seem closed, and then they seem permeable. The spectator becomes an integral protagonist in the event. The way of light and shadow during the day characterizes the image."

Almost in the center of this slightly staggered build-

ing is the main entrance in a narrow gap in the glass — "shaped like a crevasse it goes through the concrete hull." This entrance leads to the flight of steps and a view of the four storeys of the seven level, 3200 sq. meter (about 33,800 sq. ft.) construction. "The stiffening beam structure repeats the style of the sloping stairs and is based on diagonals resulting in triangles and rhombi. A second entrance leads directly to the second floor with its panoramic glass front via a ramp-like flight of stairs. This has a double effect: an improved frequency of the shopping storeys, plus an additional opportunity for communication." The interior design of Brundl "repeats this methodology and interprets the geometry of the façade." The structure finds hold in the core of granite that stretches across all the stories,

By means of the broken up roof and the view outside, "the artificially created landscape of the shopping world picks up the thread of the real landscape." Christoph Brundl adds, "To us the view

outside up to the very particular mountain scenery and the Kaprun River is a very special aspect."

Spread out throughout this exciting architectural space is everything the outdoors enthusiast could hope to find — all beautifully merchandised and illuminated. Textures like natural stone and stacked lumber complement the smooth, slick surfaces and the many glazed areas that allow the daylight and the fabulous scenery into the geometrically contrived space. Walls are finished in graphite brick and deep brushed oak, while exposed concrete is visible on some walls and on the ceilings. Bolidt select soft and Bolidft fifty fifty (thermo hardened plastics) cover the floors and steel and concrete stairways connect the different levels. There is a charming café/restaurant on the upper level where shoppers can relax, indulge and get instant gratification in the view-filled surround.

The new Brundl is "a very daring, polarizing urban architecture partially provoking the typical lederhosen setting" says Mr. Brundl. For him "it is as if the building breathes." It not only links shopping with adventure but does create a place for communication between people and the out of doors.

Nike iD Studio

Niketown, London, UK

DESIGN
Nike Brand Design, HMKM

FIXTURES
Umdasch Shop Concepts,
Amstetten, Austria

PHOTOGRAPHY
Katrien Franken

Of special interest in the London flagship Niketown store is a new area which was created to help re-launch the Nike brand in Europe. It is the Nike iD Studio where customers can design their own Nike shoes on the software that is provided on the first level of this new shop.

According to the Umdasch Shopfitters who design-ed and produced the fixtures for this shop it "is in the shape of a suspended glass and steel cube, in which there are two sales levels and where customers can have running shoes made to measure. The various levels are interconnected by means of bridges." This studio is located in a covered inner courtyard of the 31,500 plus sq. ft. Niketown structure.

In addition to the software, previously mentioned, on the first level there is also a selection of materials, colors and labels. The spacious consultation areas are in the central space and the glass shelves on the rear wall are visible from both inside and outside the Studio and help to focus attention onto the sport shoes.

The second level of the cube "offers more exclusivity" and here shoppers may make an appointment to meet and consult with a professional designer at "the teacher's table." A mixture of walnut veneer, polished stainless steel and white steel, plus gleaming black and white surfaces give the shop a space age feel. The occasional burst of red orange on an over scaled graphic or a column enclosure enlivens the look of the otherwise stark and dramatic look.

The low lighting and the lustrous black fixtures plus the floating glass shelves all contribute to the special shopping experience the client gets at Nike iD. Numerous small metal halide lamps light up the hundreds of shoes displayed on the glass shelves that hug the glass perimeter walls while a few others add dramatically to the ambient light. Some of the fixtures, such as the central counter, are illuminated from below, contributing to the "floating feeling" of the Studio design.

"The design of the Nike store is one of the boldest examples of interior design in London and corresponds with the visual merchandising." The bold and striking new Nike iD Studio was one of the prize winners of the Euro Shop Retail awards.

L.L.Bean

Dedham, MA

DESIGN
Bergmeyer, Boston MA

The Bergmeyer design firm had created a prototype concept for free standing L.L.Bean stores. The new Outdoor Lifestyle store that opened in Dedham follows and expands on that design. "The goal of this project was to create a unique store experience focusing on celebrating the rich history and heritage of L.L.Bean while showcasing the brand's outdoor lifestyle products." To amplify the brand's philosophy—"Learn, Try, Buy, Enjoy"—this store's exterior and interior design encourages shoppers to make it "an educational experience" by touching, trying and getting involved with the products.

From its wood and glass exterior to its wood enhanced interior, this multi-level store looks like a "cabin in the woods" as imagined by a creative, modern architect. The use of natural materials, the abundance of light streaming in through the generous amounts of glass and the focus on energy conservation—all part of the company's commitment to environmental stewardship—contribute to the look and feel of the space.

There is also the feeling of a western town as imaged in the cowboy movies of the 1940s and '50s—updated and cleaned up—in the wood façade especially with the covered walkway leading to the entrance to the shop. The giant L.L.Bean boot—enlarged to 12 ft.—identifies the store as do the illuminated logo signs on the facade. Upon entering, the feeling of space is overwhelming as one walks into the open area and can see the whole of the wood slat sided banister that accentuates the twisting staircase that connects with the mezzanine above. A similar "fence" of assorted width slats of wood encompasses this upper level

where the outdoor fashions are shown. The small canoes/boats hanging over the railing add bright touches of color to the otherwise wood-toned surround. Aisles covered with recycled rubber material lead shoppers around on both levels while grass-green carpeting is underfoot in the merchandised and outdoor themed areas. Some walls are covered with a horizontal slat wall system for merchandise display while floor fixtures, made of wood and metal, underscore the "rustic," "natural" and "outdoorsy" concept of the store design. As one walks the store the original impression of openness recedes and individual areas become more intimate and human in scale.

This is another project for L.L.Bean that is LEED Certified. It contains many sustainable design elements, from the materials used to the use of natural light and energy efficient techniques—all to satisfy L.L.Bean's commitment

to sustainability. The custom made fixtures were fabricated of reclaimed wood and steel. The lighting program was refined to ensure that the innovative lighting control system took advantage of the natural light and reduced the store's overall energy consumption. Recycled content carpet and rubber flooring, reclaimed wood for wall panels, FSC (Forest Stewardship Certified) new wood products made of readily replenishable woods, and paints and adhesives containing minimal organic compounds were also used on this project.

This is a store that is mostly brown and beige — yet "green" all over.

The Flagship Store Powered by Reebok

MetLife Stadium, East Rutherford, NJ

DESIGN
Chute Gerdeman, Columbus, OH

FOUNDER / CEO
Denny Gerdeman

PRESIDENT / CHIEF CREATIVE DIRECTOR
Brian Shafley

EVP, ACCOUNT MANAGEMENT
Wendy Johnson

CREATIVE DIRECTOR, BRAND COMMUNICATIONS
Corey Dehus

DIRECTOR, DESIGN DEVELOPMENT
Steve Pottschmidt

SR. DESIGNER, RETAIL ENVIRONMENTS
Rob Turner

SR. DESIGNER, GRAPHIC PRODUCTION
Steve Johnson

DESIGNER AND MATERIALS SPECIALIST
Katie Clements

ARCHITECT
CG Architecture, Columbus, OH

LIGHTING TECHNOLOGY
X-nth, Maitland, FL

GENERAL CONTRACTOR
Shawmut Design & Construction, Boston, MA

PHOTOGRAPHY
Mark Steele Photography, Columbus OH

People love to collect souvenirs! They are memories that one can hold onto — to touch — long after the actual moment or event has passed. However, sports fans are a different breed of memory or souvenir shopper. They use their "souvenirs" as markers — as in-your-face signs of allegiance — of belonging and being a part of a bigger thing. They usually prefer boldly branded wear that they can layer themselves in to show the world and the people around them at a game where their hearts and minds are.

The new 9.600 sq. ft. store, designed by Chute Gerdeman of Columbus, OH in conjunction with Delaware North Companies, is truly unique. Using a combination of modern architectural design and the newest technology in lighting, the Flagship Store Powered by Reebok was created and has the capability of transforming to accommodate the two different teams that share the new MetLife Stadium in East Rutherford for their home games. Thus, Giants and Jets fans can purchase team customized wear and accessories — Giants wear when the Giants are playing or Jets branded apparel when the Jets take over the field. When neither team is "at home" the store is split 50-50 and shoppers can purchase apparel branded for either team. Donna Genesky, Director of Retail for Delaware North Sportservice said, "Our